Signaling Games in Political Science

FUNDAMENTALS OF PURE AND APPLIED ECONOMICS

EDITORS IN CHIEF

J. LESOURNE, Conservatoire National des Arts et Métiers,
Paris, France
H. SONNENSCHEIN, University of Pennsylvania
Philadelphia, Pennsylvania, USA

ADVISORY BOARD

K. ARROW, Stanford, California, USA
W. BAUMOL, Princeton, New Jersey, USA
W. A. LEWIS, Princeton, New Jersey, USA
S. TSURU, Tokyo, Japan

Fundamentals of Pure and Applied Economics in an international series of titles divided by discipline into sections. A list of sections and their editors and of published titles may be found at the back of this volume.

Signaling Games in Political Science

Jeffrey S. Banks
University of Rochester, New York, USA

A volume in the Political Science and Economics section

edited by

J. Ferejohn
Stanford University, California

h harwood academic publishers
ap chur · london · paris · new york · melbourne

© 1991 by Harwood Academic Publishers GmbH
Poststrasse 22, 7000 Chur, Switzerland
All rights reserved

Harwood Academic Publishers

Post Office Box 197	Post Office Box 786
London WC2E 9PX	Cooper Station
United Kingdom	New York, New York 10276
	United States of America
58, rue Lhomond	Private Bag 8
75005 Paris	Camberwell, Victoria 3124
France	Australia

Library of Congress Cataloging-in-Publication Data

Banks, Jeffrey S.
    Signaling games in political science/ Jeffrey S. Banks.
        p. cm. — (Fundamentals of pure and applied economics, ISSN
0191-1708; v. 46. Political science and economics section)
    Includes bibliographical references and index.
    ISBN 3-7186-5087-8
    1. Political science—Mathematical models. 2. Uncertainty—
Mathematical models. 3. Game theory. 4. Games of strategy
(Mathematics). I. Title. II. Series: Fundamentals of pure and
applied economics; v. 46. III. Series: Fundamentals of pure and
applied economics. Political science and economics section.
JA74.B34 1991
320′.01′51—dc20

91-14677
CIP

Contents

Introduction to the Series

Drawing on a personal network, an economist can still relatively easily stay well informed in the narrow field in which he works, but to keep up with the development of economics as a whole is a much more formidable challenge. Economists are confronted with difficulties associated with the rapid development of their discipline. There is a risk of "balkanization" in economics, which may not be favorable to its development.

Fundamentals of Pure and Applied Economics has been created to meet this problem. The discipline of economics has been subdivided into sections (listed at the back of this volume). These sections comprise short books, each surveying the state of the art in a given area.

Each book starts with the basic elements and goes as far as the most advanced results. Each should be useful to professors needing material for lectures, to graduate students looking for a global view of a particular subject, to professional economists wishing to keep up with the development of their science, and to researchers seeking convenient information on questions that incidentally appear in their work.

Each book is thus a presentation of the state of the art in a particular field rather than a step-by-step analysis of the development of the literature. Each is a high-level presentation but accessible to anyone with a solid background in economics, whether engaged in business, government, international organizations, teaching, or research in related fields.

Three aspects of *Fundamentals of Pure and Applied Economics* should be emphasized:

—First, the project covers the whole field of economics, not only theoretical or mathematical economics.
—Second, the project is open-ended and the number of books is not predetermined. If new interesting areas appear, they will generate additional books.

—Last, all the books making up each section will later be grouped to constitute one or several volumes of an Encyclopedia of Economics.

The editors of the sections are outstanding economists who have selected as authors for the series some of the finest specialists in the world.

J. Lesourne   *H. Sonnenschein*

SIGNALING GAMES IN POLITICAL SCIENCE*

JEFFREY S. BANKS

University of Rochester, New York

1. INTRODUCTION

In the past twenty years or so rational choice models have become a common if not completely accepted paradigm from which to generate predictions of and explanations for political behavior. These include models of electoral competition, committee behavior in legislatures, voting behavior under various sorts of agendas, international relations, public goods provision, and a host of other topics. In each of these areas the principal mode of analysis has been game-theoretic; hence a characterization of the equilibrium behavior of the participants generates both a description of the individual incentives inherent in the system as well as a subsequent conclusion about the aggregate or social outcome derived from such a system.

Until recently most of the studies have been performed using the overly restrictive but technically appealing assumption of complete information, wherein each participant knows all of the relevant decision parameters of every other participant. The restrictiveness of this assumption can be seen by the predictions associated with it, e.g. wars should never happen, commonly-observed rules in Congress should never be employed, etc., as well as the fact that the common non-game-theoretic wisdom on these subjects concluded that informational asymmetries were the very reason such phenomena persist.[1] The attractiveness of the assumption was in part a function of the limited advance of the game theory discipline: prior to Harsanyi's [41] seminal work there did not exist a well-founded theory of incomplete

*I would like to thank David Austen–Smith and Steve Matthews for valuable comments and suggestions, and the National Science Foundation and the Sloan Foundation for generous financial support.
[1] See Sections 7.1 and 3.1 below.

1

information games analogous to that which existed for games with complete information. Therefore the toolbox possessed by the rational choice analyst was incompatible with the logical underpinnings of the environments which the analyst wished to explore.

The scenario is similar to that found in economics, in particular to topics such as limit pricing and predation in models of industrial organization. For example, the old school wisdom on limit pricing was that the behavior of a monopolist transmitted information to potential entrants concerning post-entry profitability; in particular pricing below the monopoly price may be optimal if such a strategy 'signals' to the entrant that the profits from the market are relatively low and the entrant would be better off staying out (Bain [11]). Yet with a complete information model there is no room for this informational role of pre-entry pricing, since the entrants will know everything the monopolist knows, and so the game-theoretic prediction was that limit pricing could not be sustained as an equilibrium phenomenon (Friedman [35]). It was only with the advent of incomplete information games that this informational role of pricing could begin to be understood within an equilibrium framework, thereby merging the old school wisdom with the new school techniques (cf. Milgrom and Roberts [53]).

The purpose of this monograph is to survey the recent literature on incomplete information games in political science. Specifically, we will examine situations in which one or more participants possess information which is both *private*, in that other participants do not possess or cannot costlessly verify the information, and *valuable*, in that the optimality of the participants' decisions is a function of this information. In addition, we assume these informed players take actions prior to the uninformed players, thereby generating the possibility of this information being signaled from the informed to the uninformed players through the informed players' choice of actions. Hence this monograph can be viewed as a companion piece to Calvert [23], which similarly addresses the issue of incomplete information in politics but in situations that do not involve the chosen actions of the players having any informational role.

We will explore how various types of behavior or institutional settings can be seen as rational responses to the presence of informational asymmetries, as well as examine whether such settings provide the incentives necessary for equilibrium actions to be 'informative'. In all of the models we study this latter issue will be non-trivial, for the common assumption is that the preferences of the players do not coincide; hence information which is transmitted through the actions of an informed player may subsequently be used against the interests of the informed player. Equilibrium behavior in the models will thus consist of a delicate balancing of the incentives for revealing information on the part of the informed players with the optimal responses to such revelations by the uninformed players.

The remainder of the monograph is structured as follows: the next section presents the basic model underlying most of the subsequent analysis, along with a pair of detailed examples illuminating the various incentives involved in the equilibrium analysis. Section 3 examines a number of models under the rubric of 'agenda control,' where one agent, subordinate to another, is given differential control of selecting the latter's choice set; the issue is then to rationalize this control as an efficient organizational design. Section 4 looks at two models of rhetoric and debate in which the 'speeches' made by certain players may influence the actions of others through the informativeness of the speech. Section 5 considers three extensions of the standard model of two-candidate electoral competition, where candidates now possess private and valuable information which is potentially revealed through the electoral process. Section 6 explores the ability of 'leaders' to enforce their desires through the development and maintenance of a reputation for punishing disobedient behavior in either a legislative or international relations scenario. Section 7 examines models of bargaining by nations in the shadow of war, where war is socially inefficient yet occurs with positive probability due to a lack of complete informativeness in the bargaining behavior of the nations. Finally, Section 8 considers the effect of incomplete information on sequential voting processes, and shows that some procedures invariably lead to the same outcomes as with complete information, while others fall dramatically short of this mark.

2. THE BASIC MODEL

2.1. Elements of the game

Although the precise models analyzed in this monograph vary widely, there does exist a common structure to the problems which can be represented by the class of incomplete information games known as *signaling games*. Incomplete information games, which were first rigorously analyzed in Harsanyi [41], generalize the more commonly studied games of complete information by allowing players to possess differential information concerning the relationship between the actions chosen by the players and the payoffs associated with those actions. One potential difficulty with such a model is that this type of uncertainty can give rise to higher orders of uncertainty, i.e. in addition to player i knowing something about payoffs that player j does not, player j's beliefs about i's information may be uncertain to i; similarly i's beliefs about j's beliefs about i's information may be uncertain, and so on *ad infinitum*. Harsanyi's fundamental insight was in showing that if the extent of these informational asymmetries are reasonably 'small' (e.g. described by a finite set), one can use the structure and mechanics of complete information games to carry out the analysis with incomplete information as well.[2]

The canonical form of a signaling game consists of two players, labelled the sender S and the receiver R, who make their decisions sequentially. Initially S selects a message $m \in M$, after which R selects an action $a \in A$, where M and A are finite sets. The payoffs to S and R are in general a function of the message-action (m, a) chosen, as well as some information privately known by S. We denote this information as player S's *type* $t \in T$, T finite, and assume that there exists a common knowledge prior belief $p(\cdot)$ over the set T, where for all $t \in T$ $p(t) > 0$. The preferences of S and R over $T \times M \times A$ are represented by von Neumann–Morgenstern utility functions $U_S(t, m, a)$ and $U_R(t, m, a)$, respectively. The structure of the game, $\Gamma = (\{S, R\}, M, A, T, p(\cdot), U_S(\cdot), U_R(\cdot))$, is assumed to be common knowledge (Aumann [3]).[3]

Since S knows the actual type t prior to selecting a message, a *strategy for S* is a function

$$s : T \to \Delta(M),$$

where for a finite set D, $\Delta(D)$ denotes the set of probability distributions over D. We write $s(m; t)$ for the probability that S sends

---

[2] Mertens and Zamir [52] present a rigorous treatment of Harsanyi's argument; and Myerson [61] gives an excellent introduction and review of the subject.

[3] Otherwise, a player's type would incorporate this additional uncertainty as well.

the message m given that his type is t, and say that type $t \in T$ sends message $m \in M$ according to the strategy $s(\cdot)$ if $s(m; t) > 0$; when $s(\cdot)$ is understood we let $m(t)$ denote a message sent by t. The receiver R observes the message sent by S but not the type; thus a *strategy for R* is a function

$$r : M \to \Delta(A),$$

where $r(a; m)$ denotes the probability that R takes action a upon observing the message m. A message $m \in M$ induces an action $a \in A$ according to $r(\cdot)$ if $r(a; m) > 0$; given a response $r(\cdot)$ let $a(m)$ be an action induced by the message m.

We extend the utility functions U_S, U_R to the domain $\Delta(A)$ by taking expected values:

$$U_i(t, m, r) = \sum_{a \in A} U_i(t, m, r) \cdot r(a;m), i = S, R. \tag{1}$$

Similarly we can extend the function U_R to the domain $\Delta(T)$:

$$U_R(\lambda, m, r) = \sum_{t \in T} U_R(t, m, r) \cdot \lambda(t), \tag{2}$$

so that the payoff to R from the response $r \in \Delta(A)$ to the message $m \in M$, given beliefs $\lambda \in \Delta(T)$, is $U_R(\lambda, m, r)$. With this notation, then, define R's *best response correspondence* as the set of responses which maximize $U_R(\lambda, m, r)$:

$$BR(\lambda, m) = \underset{r \in \Delta(A)}{\text{argmax}} \ U_R(\lambda, m, r). \tag{3}$$

For any $\wedge \subset \Delta(T)$ let $BR(\wedge, m) = \cup_{\lambda \in \wedge} BR(\lambda, m)$ be the set of optimal responses when R's beliefs are restricted to the set $\wedge$. For notational simplicity define $BR(m) \equiv BR(\Delta(T), m)$ as the set of *all* possible best responses following the message m.

In certain situations it is useful to re-scale the payoffs of the players in a manner which preserves the decision-theoretic properties of the game. It is well known that in complete information games the von Neumann–Morgenstern utility representations of players' preferences are only unique up to an increasing linear transformation. Hence if player i has a VN-M utility function u_i over the product of players' strategy spaces, then i's behavior in the game will be equivalent to that generated if his preferences were represented by $\tilde{u}_i = c_i \cdot u_i + d_i$, $c_i > 0$. With signaling games the assumption is that the sender knows the value of t prior to selecting a message; hence we can make such a re-scaling of $U_S(\cdot)$ 'type-by-type', since the particular re-scaling of one type can in no way effect the behavior of the sender if she is another type. Thus we say a *utility equivalent* (Myerson [61]) transformation of a signaling game occurs if we replace $U_S(t, m, a)$ and $U_R(t, m, a)$ with

$$\tilde{U}_S(t, m, a) = c_S(t) \cdot U_S(t, m, a) + d_S(t), \ c_S(t) > 0, \qquad (4)$$

and

$$\tilde{U}_R(t, m, a) = c_R \cdot U_R(t, m, a) + d_R, \ c_R > 0, \qquad (5)$$

respectively.

2.2. Equilibrium behavior

As with most rational choice models we analyze signaling games by identifying equilibrium behavior on the part of the sender and the receiver. The most widely employed equilibrium concept in signaling games is that of sequential equilibrium (Kreps and Wilson [46]), where this concept differs from most other equilibrium concepts (e.g. Nash, perfect, proper) in that a sequential equilibrium explicitly characterizes the beliefs of the players concerning the history of play at any point in the decision making process. For signaling games this is quite natural, for the only such uncertainty is the receiver's belief about the sender's type, where this belief can differ according to the message observed by R. Thus a sequential equilibrium consists of strategies (s, r), as well as posterior beliefs for R

$$\mu : M \to \Delta(T),$$

where $\mu(t; m)$ is the receiver's belief about the likelihood the sender is type t given that R has observed the message m. These beliefs then allow the receiver to evaluate the optimality of any response to a given message by computing the expected utility of that action, where this expectation is with respect to the belief μ.

Definition.
A *sequential equilibrium* of a signaling game is a triple (s^*, r^*, μ^*), where

(i) $\forall t \in T$, $s^*(m'; t) > 0$ only if

$m' \in \underset{m \in M}{\operatorname{argmax}} \ U_S(t, m, r^*(m))$;

(ii) $\forall m \in M$, $r^*(a'; m) > 0$ only if

$a' \in \underset{a \in A}{\operatorname{argmax}} \ U_R(\mu^*(m), m, a)$;

(iii) $\forall m \in M$ such that $\sum_{t \in T} s^*(m; t) > 0$, $\mu^*(m)$ satisfies

$$\mu^*(t'; m) = \frac{s^*(m; t') \cdot p(t')}{\sum_{t \in T} s^*(m; t) \cdot p(t)}$$

Condition (i) requires S's strategy to be optimal given R's strategy; in particular, for each type $t \in T$, $m^*(t)$ must be a best response to r^*, where $m^*(t)$ is a message sent by t according to $s^*(\cdot)$. This implies the sender will only randomize and send more than one message with positive probability if all such messages generate the same expected utility. Condition (ii) requires R's strategy to be optimal given beliefs μ^*, so for each message $m \in M$ an action $a^*(m)$ induced by m according to $r^*(\cdot)$ must maximize the receiver's expected utility. Finally, condition (iii) requires R's beliefs μ^* to be 'consistent' with S's strategy s^*, in that for all messages m sent with positive probability by some type $\mu^*(\cdot; m)$ satisfies Bayes' Rule according to the prior belief p and the strategy s^*.

Condition (iii) implies, for example, that if according to $s^*(\cdot)$ only type t' sends message m', and t' only sends m', then upon observing m' R should place probability 1 on S's type being t'. In this sense we say that t' *separates* according to the strategy $s^*(\cdot)$, in that R is able to distinguish t' from all other types of sender; $s^*(\cdot)$ is then a separating strategy if all types separate. On the other hand if t and t' both only send m', and are the only types that send m', then R's posterior belief upon observing m' places positive probability only on t and t', so that $\mu(t'; m') = p(t')/[p(t') + p(t)]$, and $\mu(t; m') = 1 - \mu(t'; m')$. In this case we say that t and t' *pool* at m', and refer to the strategy $s^*(\cdot)$ as a pooling strategy if all types pool with each other at some message m'. Thus if all types pool at m' the posterior belief of R upon observing m' is simply equal to the prior belief. In general, the receiver's posterior beliefs concerning the sender's type upon observing messages sent in equilibrium, i.e. $m \in M$ such that $\Sigma_{t \in T} s^*(m; t) > 0$, are determined by the sender's strategy $s^*(\cdot)$, which gives the relative likelihood that a type sends a particular message, and the prior belief $p(\cdot)$.

From the definition above it is clear that for signaling games the receiver's beliefs at 'out-of-equilibrium' messages, i.e. $m \in M$ such that $\Sigma_{t \in T} s^*(m; t) = 0$, are not restricted in any way by the sequential equilibrium concept; the only requirement is that the receiver possess *some* belief concerning the sender's type, and then optimize accordingly. This definition differs from the Bayesian equilibrium concept due to Harsanyi [41], which simply requires optimality by the receiver along the equilibrium path. Bayesian equilibrium then allows R to take actions out of equilibrium which are never best responses, for example dominated actions, whereas sequential equilibrium requires $a^*(m) \in BR(m)$. Thus if we modify condition ii) in the definition of sequential equilibrium by replacing '$\forall m \in M$' with '$\forall m \in M$ such that $\Sigma_{t \in T} s^*(m; t) > 0$' we would have the definition of Bayesian equilibrium for signaling games.

Although sequential equilibrium places no restrictions on out of equilibrium beliefs in signaling games, it is also true that many of the games analyzed below are not strictly speaking signaling games, and in some of these the more general definition of 'consistent' beliefs from Kreps and Wilson [46] does have some impact. In particular, suppose we consider a model with a single sender but multiple receivers $R_1, \ldots, R_n$, all of whom select their actions simultaneously upon observing the message choice by the sender. Sequential equilibrium then implies that the receivers' beliefs be the limit of a sequence of beliefs derived via Bayes' Rule from a sequence of completely mixed strategies by S (i.e. $s(m; t) > 0 \forall m \in M, \forall t \in T$), where this sequence converges to the equilibrium strategy $s^*(\cdot)$. Since a single sequence defines the beliefs for all of the receivers, their beliefs coincide along this sequence, and hence in its limit. Therefore with multiple receivers the sequential equilibrium concept requires that all receivers possess the same beliefs in *and* out of equilibrium. Such a condition, while arguably quite restrictive, renders the analysis in certain variants of signaling games considered below reasonably tractable.

There exists a certain similarity between a separating equilibrium in a signaling game and the equilibrium of the game if there were no incomplete information, i.e. where there exists a type $t \in T$ such that $p(t) = 1$. By definition a separating equilibrium induces a response by the receiver which is optimal given the sender's true type, and so R's actions along the equilibrium path are consistent with the complete information environment. Yet it is possible that S's separating message will differ from the complete information equilibrium message,[4] since in a separating equilibrium the messages must be such that no type prefers to send some other type's message. Indeed, it is easily shown that, regardless of type, the sender's equilibrium utility in a separating equilibrium must be no greater than that with complete information. The argument is as follows: let $m(t)$ be the sender's message if type t; by separation this leads to a response $a(m(t))$ which is optimal given beliefs $\mu(t; m) = 1$. Now with complete information the message $m(t)$ would be followed by the same action $a(m(t))$, since t is known; hence with complete information S can always get as least as high a payoff as in a separating equilibrium with incomplete information by simply sending $m(t)$. Any discrepancy in these payoffs can then be described as the 'incentive costs' of separation incurred by a type t sender.

On the other hand a pooling equilibrium in a signaling game resembles behavior in a game where neither the receiver *nor* the sender knows the value of t, since now R's equilibrium response to a pooled message m is identical to that when S does not know t and hence cannot condition the choice of message on t. The same revealed preference argument as above then shows that regardless of type, the sender's payoff in a pooling equilibrium is no greater than it would be *ex post* if S did not know t: in the latter situation S can still choose m and receive the same response as in the pooling equilibrium, implying S cannot be any worse off without the information. And, as above, the payoffs from the pooling equilibrium may be strictly lower due to the presence of incentive costs, where now these occur in order to provide the incentive for S in essence to ignore the private information and act the same regardless of type.

2.3. An example with two types: the Spence model

As an example of sequential equilibrium analysis in signaling games, we consider the model of job market signaling due to Spence [78], which initiated the study of signaling games in economics.[5] A worker

---

[4] For simplicity assume this equilibrium is unique.
[5] See also Riley [69].

can be one of two types, $T = \{1,2\}$, and selects a level of education $m \in \mathbb{R}_+$; let $p \in (0, 1)$ denote the prior probability the worker is type 1. Two identical risk-neutral firms, i and j, observe the worker's education choice, but not her type, and then simultaneously offer wages for her employment a_i, a_j, respectively. The worker then selects the firm offering the highest wage, randomizing if $a_i = a_j$. Letting $a = \max\{a_i, a_j\}$, the payoff to the worker, the sender in this model, from selecting education level m given type t and wage a, is

$$U_S(t, m, a) = a - m^2/t. \tag{6}$$

Therefore the worker experiences a disutility associated with education, where this disutility is lower for higher types. For the firms, the productivity of a type t worker who selects education level m is $t.m$, so the payoff to firm i from attracting a type t worker with education level m with a wage a_i is simply

$$U_{R_i}(t, m, a_i) = t.m - a_i; \tag{7}$$

if firm i does not attract the worker then its payoff is equal to zero.

From the previous subsection we know that in a sequential equilibrium the firms' beliefs about the worker's type upon observing education level m will be identical regardless of whether m is sent in equilibrium; this plus the 'Bertrand' bidding for the worker's services imply that for any posterior belief μ and education level m, in equilibrium the firms will both offer

$$a(\mu, m) = \sum_T \mu(t, m)t.m = \mu(1, m)m + (1 - \mu(1, m))2m. \tag{8}$$

In particular, for all $m \in \mathbb{R}$, $a(\mu, m) \in [m, 2m]$ for all μ, i.e. the least the firms will pay will be value associated with a type 1 worker and the most will be that associated with a type 2 worker.

Next we turn to a characterization of equilibrium behavior in the model. As noted in subsection 2.2 there exists a certain degree of latitude in specifying out-of-equilibrium beliefs in any sequential equilibrium, and therefore our interest is not really a characterization of all sequential equilibria but rather a characterization of the set of sequential equilibrium *paths*, i.e. equilibrium messages and the resulting equilibrium wages. With this as the goal we can without loss of generality let the firms' beliefs be $\mu(1, m') = 1$ for all $m' \notin \{s(1), s(2)\}$;

thus the firms' out-of-equilibrium beliefs are always that the worker is of type 1, and hence the wage associated with m' is simply m', the lowest possible value. Such beliefs are clearly the 'strongest', in that if there exists a sequential equilibrium where for some out-of-equilibrium message m' $\mu(1, m') < 1$ then there will exist another equilibrium with $\mu(1, m') = 1$ which generates the same equilibrium path: if types 1 and 2 did not have an incentive to send m' in the former case then they will not have an incentive in the latter, since the wage is strictly lower. Therefore setting $\mu(1, m') = 1$ will generate all of the possible sequential equilibrium paths.

Let $m^c(t)$ denote the optimal education level of a type t worker in the complete information game where t is known to both firms:

$$m^c(t) = \operatorname*{argmax}_{m} t.m - m^2/t. \tag{9}$$

Our first constraint is that in any sequential equilibrium, the worker's utility if type 1 must be at least as great as $U_S(1, m^c(1), m^c(1))$, her equilibrium complete information payoff. This follows since by selecting $m = m^c(1)$ the worker is guaranteed a wage of $at\ least\ m^c(1)$ by the above restriction on the firms' optimal behavior. Alternatively, let $m(2, 1)$ denote the message which maximizes the worker's utility given type 2 when the firm's beliefs following $every$ message is $\mu(1, m) = 1$. Then by the same logic, in any equilibrium a type 2 worker's utility will be at least $U_S(2, m(2, 1), m(2, 1))$, since for each education level a worker will get a wage of at least m. Let $\underline{U}(1)$, $\underline{U}(2)$ denote these minimal levels of equilibrium utility for the sender of each type. Then it is easily seen that $m(2, 1) > m^c(1)$, and that the indifference curves in (m, a)–space associated with the worker's different types are as in Figure 1.

Consider first the existence of separating equilibria in the model, i.e. where $m(t)$ is unique and $m(1) \neq m(2)$. By separation, then, $\mu(t, m(t)) = 1$, and the equilibrium wage will be on the $a = m$ line for $t = 1$ and the $a = 2m$ line for $t = 2$. By the above restriction on a type 1's payoff, in any separating equilibrium $m(1)$ must be equal to $m^c(1)$. As for the separating message of a type 2 worker, from Figure 1 it is clear that any such message must be greater than m_a, since otherwise a type 1 worker would prefer the (m, a)–pair $(m(2), 2m(2))$ to $(m(1), 2m(1))$. In addition, $m(2)$ must be less than m_b, since otherwise a type 2 worker would prefer to send $m(2, 1)$ regardless of the response to such a message.

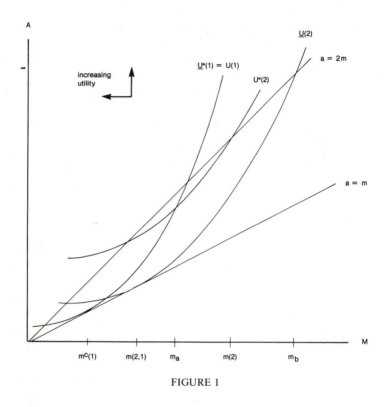

FIGURE 1

It turns out that *any* message $m \in |m_a, m_b]$ can be supported as the separating message of a type 2 worker in a sequential equilibrium, given the assumption $\mu(1, m') = 1$ for all $m' \neq m(2)$. Since $m(2)$ is less than m_b, a type 2 worker will not have an incentive to send $m(2, 1)$, and since by assumption $m(2, 1)$ maximizes a type 2 worker's payoff over all $m \neq m(2)$ she will not have an incentive to send any other message as well. A similar conclusion holds for a type 1 worker, since $m(2)$ is greater than m_a and $m^c(1)$ maximizes type 1's utility over all $m \neq m(2)$. Thus there exists a continuum of separating equilibrium paths in the two-type Spence model, parameterized by the message sent by the type 2 worker.

Now consider the existence of pooling equilibria in the model; i.e. where $m(1) = m(2) = m^*$. At m^* then the firms' equilibrium posterior belief is simply equal to their prior belief, so the equilibrium wage is

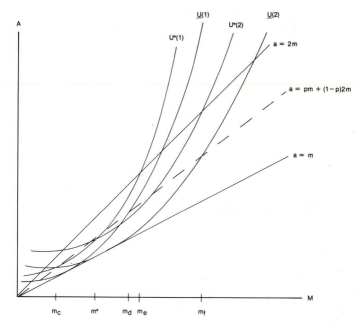

FIGURE 2

simply $p.m^* + (1 - p)2m^*$. By the above assumption, let $\mu(1, m') = 1$ for all $m' \neq m^*$. Then, as long as $(m^*, a(p, m^*))$ is on a higher indifference curve for both types than their 'minimal' indifference curves $U(1)$, $U(2)$, m^* will be an equilibrium pooled message. Thus from Figure 2 there will be a continuum of pooling equilibria in the two-type Spence model, parameterized by the pooled message m^*, where m^* lies in the interval $[m_c, m_d]$.

Finally, there also exist semi-pooling equilibria, where type 1 sends both $m^c(1)$ and m^* with positive probability, while type 2 sends m^* with probability 1; if $s(1, m^*) = s$, then Bayes' Rule implies the firms' beliefs at m^* is $\mu(1, m^*) = s.p/[s.p + (1 - p)]$. Since s must be between 0 and 1, the equilibrium wage offered at m^* will fall between $p.m^* + (1 - p)2m^*$ and $2m^*$. In addition, for a type 1 worker to be sending both $m^c(1)$ and m^* with positive probability, the pair $(m^*, a(\mu(1, m^*), m^*))$ must lie on the $U(1)$ indifference curve; see Figure 3. Therefore, m^* will be in the interval $[m_d, m_a]$, and for each message in this interval there exists a unique value of s generating the

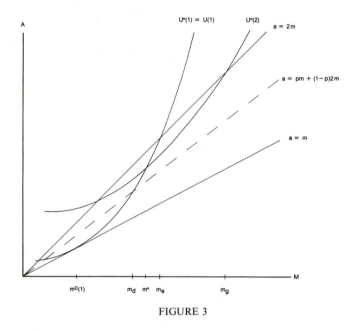

FIGURE 3

required posterior probability and resulting wage. Now as before set $\mu(1, m') = 1$ for all $m' \neq m^*$; then in the two-type Spence model there exists a continuum of semi-pooling equilibria, parameterized by the common message m^*.

2.4. Equilibrium refinements

From the above example it is clear that one potential difficulty with analyzing signaling games is the presence of multiple equilibria. With complete information (i.e. $p = 0$ or $p = 1$) there is a unique sequential equilibrium, whereas with incomplete information we have separating equilibria, pooling equilibria, and semi-pooling equilibria, and even within each of these classes there exist a multitude of equilibria. Hence in terms of generating behavioral predictions in signaling games the sequential equilibrium concept can be quite weak; in particular, *any* message between m_c (from Figure 2) and m_b (from Figure 1) is predicted according to *some* sequential equilibrium. This has led various authors to propose refinements of sequential equilibrium for signaling games (cf. Cho and Kreps [25], Banks and Sobel [18], Grossman and Perry [39]), where rather than imposing, e.g. a Pareto criterion to compare and select among the equilibria (cf. Harsanyi [42]) these refinements constrain the one 'free variable' remaining in the definition of sequential equilibrium, namely the out-of-equilibrium beliefs of the receiver, to generate more restrictive equilibrium concepts. Thus, whereas sequential equilibrium refines Bayesian equilibrium by requiring out-of-equilibrium *actions* to be consistent with some posterior belief over T, the concepts we outline below refine the sequential equilibrium concept by requiring the out-of-equilibrium *beliefs* to be consistent with a particular criterion. Rather than go through all of these criteria, we will outline the few relevant criteria for the models analyzed in this monograph.

Let (s^*, r^*, μ^*) be a sequential equilibrium, $U^*(t) \equiv U_S(t, m^*, r^*(m^*))$ (where m^* is such that $s^*(m^*; t) > 0$) be the equilibrium expected utility of S when her type is t, and suppose the message $m \in M$ is out-of-equilibrium, i.e. $\Sigma_{t \in T} s^*(m, t) = 0$. The weakest refinement of sequential equilibrium we consider, the *intuitive criterion* due to Cho and Kreps [25], says the following: suppose $U^*(t)$ is greater than the payoff S would receive if type t sent message m for any possible best response by the receiver, $U^*(t) > \max_{r \in BR(m)} U_S(t, m, r)$; further, assume there exists a type t' where this does not hold. Then the posterior belief at m should place zero probability on type t: $\mu^*(t, m) = 0$. The logic of this criterion (as well as those to follow) is that out-of-equilibrium messages should be viewed by the receiver as possible 'defections' from the equilibrium play of the game. Hence in constructing his posterior belief at such a message R should judge the willingness of different sender types to send this message relative to behaving according to the equilibrium prediction. This then requires the posterior belief of the receiver to be rational with regard to the incentives for defection on the part of the sender, thereby linking out-of-equilibrium beliefs with equilibrium payoffs. Thus if $U^*(t) > \max_{r \in BR(m)} U_S(t, m, r)$ the receiver should reasonably conclude that a type t sender would never defect to the previously unsent message m. Further, this requirement should hold for all out-of-equilibrium messages, so that we say a sequential equilibrium is *intuitive* if for all messages $m \in M$ such that $\Sigma_{t \in T} s^*(m, t) = 0$, $\mu(t, m) > 0$ only if $U^*(t) < \max_{r \in BR(m)} U_S(t, m, r)$.

As Cho and Kreps [25] show, the intuitive criterion eliminates all but a single sequential equilibrium path in the two-type Spence model. To see this, consider a separating equilibrium in Figure 1 where $m(2) > m_a$ and $m(2) \neq m^c(2)$, and consider an out-of-equilibrium message $m' \in (m_a, m(2))$. Then clearly $U^*(1) > \max_{a\in[m, 2m]} U_S(1, m', a)$ while $U^*(2) < \max_{a\in[m, 2m]} U_S(2, m', a)$; thus the intuitive criterion requires $\mu(2, m') = 1$. This then implies a wage equal to $2m'$ which induces a type 2 worker to deviate to m', thereby upsetting the equilibrium. Continuing to apply this logic, we see that the only intuitive separating equilibrium is where $m(2) = \max\{m^c(2), m_a\}$, i.e. either a type 2 worker sends her complete information optimal message, or (if $m^c(2) < m_a$) the message where a type 1 worker is just indifferent between sending $m^c(1)$ and $m(2)$. Similarly, for any out-of-equilibrium message $m' \in (m_e, m_f)$ for the pooling equilibrium or $m' \in (m_a, m_g)$ for the semi-pooling equilibrium, the intuitive criterion requires $\mu(2, m') = 1$ and therefore a wage $2m'$, thus upsetting the equilibrium.

Hence we see how the intuitive criterion, while apparently a weak requirement on out-of-equilibrium beliefs of the receiver, is sufficient to select a unique equilibrium path in the Spence model with two types. With regard to the models considered here, the intuitive criterion is sufficient to generate unique behavioral predictions in the two-type reputations models of Calvert [24] and Alt, Calvert, and Humes [2]. However Cho and Kreps [25] also show that this uniqueness result in the Spence model fails to hold when the worker can be of more than two types, thereby necessitating a stronger refinement concept for uniqueness. Cho and Kreps [25] and Banks and Sobel [18] propose a variety of such criteria; however it turns out that in numerous signaling games, including most of the ones considered here, these criteria are equivalent, and also equivalent to the even stronger notion of stable equilibria due to Kohlberg and Mertens [45].[6] For example, the concept known as *D1* (Cho and Kreps [25]) requires the following: suppose that at the out-of-equilibrium message m there exists types t, t' such that for all responses r where $U^*(t) \leq U_S(t, m, r)$, $U^*(t') < U_S(t', m, r)$, implying whenever type t weakly prefers to defect to m type t' strictly prefers to defect. Then *D1* requires the posterior belief at m to place zero probability on type t, since t' is 'more likely' to defect to m than t. Formally, a sequential equilibrium satisfies *D1* if for all out-of-equilib-

---

[6] Cho and Sobel [26] provide sufficient conditions on player preferences for this equivalence of equilibrium concepts to exist.

rium messages m, $\mu(t, m) > 0$ only if for all $t' \neq t$ there exists a response $r \in BR(m)$ such that $U^*(t) < U_S(t, m, r)$ while $U^*(t') \geq U_S(t', m, r)$.

Alternatively, *universal divinity* (Banks and Sobel [18]) or *D2* (Cho and Kreps [25]) would require $\mu(t, m) = 0$ if for all responses r where $U^*(t) \leq U_S(t, m, r)$ there exists a type t' such that $U^*(t') < U_S(t', m, r)$. Thus under universal divinity it need not be the *same* type which is more likely to defect for all responses.[7] A sequential equilibrium satisfies universal divinity then if for all out-of-equilibrium messages m, $\mu(t, m) > 0$ only if there exists a response $r \in BR(m)$ such that $U^*(t) < U_S(t, m, r)$ and $U^*(t') \geq U_S(t', m, r)$ for all $t' \neq t$.

The rationale for why *D1* and universal divinity tend to coincide in signaling games is derived from the common underlying monotonicity of the sender's preferences. This monotonicity then typically implies that the sets of responses providing the incentives to deviate will be nested by type; therefore *D1* and universal divinity will be equivalent. For example, in the Spence model all worker types prefer higher wages to lower. Thus, at an out-of-equilibrium message m one can identify the wage $a \in \mathbb{R}$ making a type t worker indifferent between defecting and remaining along the equilibrium path; by the above monotonicity in wages, then, any higher wage would imply a strict preference for defecting. Thus by identifying the types who have the lowest 'indifference wage' at m, we will have the types most likely to defect. Both *D1* and universal divinity then require posterior beliefs to place positive probability only on these types. In the next subsection we apply universal divinity to the Spence model with a continuum of types.

In general, then, the equilibrium refinements outlined above can be useful tools in selecting from the set of sequential equilibria those that satisfy more stringent rationality requirements.[8] Further, if the sets T, M, A are finite then existence of, e.g. a universally divine equilibrium is guaranteed (Banks and Sobel [18]).[9]

---

[7] The actual definition of universal divinity is somewhat more involved, but this characterization is sufficient for the models in this monograph.

[8] This is not to imply the use of equilibrium refinements is without controversy. For example, debate continues on whether normal form or extensive form representations, and their associated equilibrium notions, is preferable; see Kohlberg and Mertens [45].

[9] Interestingly, there exist examples which show that these refinements may run counter to the Pareto criterion relative to the set of sequential equilibria; see Banks and Sobel [19].

2.5. Two examples of continuous-type signaling games

Suppose that we alter the Spence model from Section 2.3 to allow for a continuum of possible worker types: $T = [\underline{t}, \overline{t}] \subset \mathbb{R}_+$. Without loss of generality we can restrict attention to pure strategies for S, so let $m(t)$ denote the education level selected by the worker if her type is t, and let $a(t)$ be the resulting equilibrium wage, where the relationship between the message m and the wage a is left implicit. The following Lemma shows that in any equilibrium the strategy $m(t)$ will be 'well-behaved'.

Lemma.
In any sequential equilibrium, $m(t)$ will be weakly monotone increasing on T.

The proof of the Lemma follows from consideration of constraints on the sender's equilibrium behavior known as *incentive compatibility* constraints (cf. d'Aspremont and Gerard–Varet [29], Myerson [60]). In equilibrium it must be that no type t can obtain a strictly higher payoff by emulating the behavior of another type, say t'. Thus, in equilibrium for all t, $t' \in T$ the following inequalities must hold:

$$a(t) - [m(t)]^2/t \geq a(t') - [m(t')]^2/t \qquad (10)$$

$$a(t') - [m(t')]^2/t' \geq a(t) - [m(t)]^2/t'. \qquad (11)$$

Subtracting the *RHS* of (11) from the *LHS* of (10), and the *LHS* of (11) from the *RHS* of (10), implies

$$[m(t)]^2 [1/t' - 1/t \geq [m(t')]^2 [1/t' - 1/t]. \qquad (12)$$

If $t > t'$, then $m(.) \geq 0$ implies $m(t) \geq m(t')$, thus proving the Lemma.

Monotonicity implies differentiability almost everywhere (Royden [73]), so that for almost all $t \in T$, either $\partial m/\partial t = 0$ or $\partial m/\partial t > 0$. In the former case $m(.)$ is a (locally) pooling strategy, since an interval of types send the same message, whereas in the latter case $m(.)$ is separating. It is also easily seen that in any sequential equilibrium $a(t)$ is weakly increasing on T, and $U_S(t, m(t), a(t))$ is increasing and continuous on T.

To see whether there exists a separating equilibrium in the model, we adopt the 'incentive compatibility' approach of Mailath [49]. Note that eq. (10) holds with equality at $t' = t$; therefore, for almost all t, the following 'local' incentive compatibility condition must hold:

$$\left. \frac{\partial U(t, m(t'), a(t'))}{\partial t'} \right|_{t'=t} = 0. \tag{13}$$

Otherwise a sender of type t could emulate the behavior of a type arbitrarily nearby and receive a strictly higher payoff. Writing out this equation,

$$\frac{\partial a}{\partial t} - 2m(t)\frac{\partial m}{\partial t}\frac{1}{t} = 0. \tag{14}$$

Now where $\partial m/\partial t = 0$ it must be that $\partial a/\partial t = 0$ as well, since locally types are pooling. On the other hand if $\partial m/\partial t > 0$, then the sender is separating, in which case $a(t) = t.m(t)$, implying $\partial a/\partial t = m(t) + t.\partial m/\partial t$. Therefore, a necessary condition for $m(.)$ to be a separating equilibrium is that it satisfy local incentive compatibility, or

$$\frac{\partial m}{\partial t} = \frac{m(t)}{2m(t)/t - t}. \tag{15}$$

From Mailath [49], we see that the preferences of the sender are such that (15) is also sufficient, implying the solution to (15) generates a family of incentive compatible strategies, i.e. strategies in which no type has an incentive to send another type's message. In addition, as in the two-type case there exists a boundary restriction implied by the sequential rationality of the firms, namely $m(\underline{t}) = m^c(\underline{t})$. Finally, by setting $\mu(\underline{t}, m) = 1$ for all $m < m^c(\underline{t})$ and $\mu(\bar{t}, m)$ for all $m > m(\bar{t})$ it is easily shown that no type has an incentive to send a message $m \notin [m(\underline{t}), m(\bar{t})]$.

Hence the solution to eq. (15) along with the constraint $m(\underline{t}) = m^c(\underline{t})$ characterizes the unique separating sequential equilibrium in the continuous-type Spence model. In addition, it is immediate that for all $t \in (\underline{t}, \bar{t}]$, $m(t) > m^c(t)$, i.e. the presence of incomplete information leads all types except the lowest to select strictly higher education levels than they would otherwise. In the language of subsection 2.2, all types except the lowest incur an incentive cost to separation.

As in the two-type case, there also exist pooling equilibria, as well as equilibria that have some pooling segments and some separating segments. However, applying the universal divinity criterion outlined in the previous subsection it is easily shown that the only such equilibrium corresponds to the unique separating equilibrium derived above.

To see this, let $m(.)$ be an equilibrium sender strategy, with corresponding equilibrium wages $a(.)$, let m be an out-of-equilibrium message, and define $w(t, m)$ as the wage which makes a type t sender indifferent between staying along the equilibrium path and deviating to m. Thus, $w(t, m)$ solves

or
$$a(t) - [m(t)]^2/t = w - m^2/t, \qquad (16)$$

$$w(t, m) = a(t) - [m(t)]^2/t + m^2/t. \qquad (17)$$

Since in any sequential equilibrium $U^*(t)$ will be differentiable almost everywhere and continuous everywhere in t, so will $w(t, \dot{m})$. Differentiating, we get

$$\frac{\partial w}{\partial t} = \frac{\partial a}{\partial t} - \{2m(t).t.\partial m/\partial t - [m(t)^2]\}/t^2 - m^2/t^2 \qquad (18)$$

$$= \left[\frac{\partial a}{\partial t} - \{2.m(t).\partial m/\partial t\} + \{[m(t)]\right]^2 - m^2\}/t^2. \qquad (19)$$

By eq. (14), the first bracketed term in (19) is zero, implying

$$\frac{\partial w}{\partial t} \gtrless 0 \text{ as } m(t) \gtrless m. \qquad (20)$$

Now since $m(.)$ is monotone increasing, it has at most a finite number of jump discontinuities. Suppose $m(.)$ has a jump at t', and $m \in ((m(t' - \epsilon), m(t' + \epsilon))$; then by continuity $t' = \text{argmin } w(t, m)$, so that universal divinity requires $\mu(t', m) = 1$. Further, if $m(t' - \epsilon)$ is a pooled message, then the equilibrium wage associated with it is strictly less than $t'.m(t' - \epsilon)$; thus by sending a message arbitrarily close to $m(t' - \epsilon)$ type t' receives a strictly higher payoff than the equilibrium payoff, thereby upsetting the equilibrium. A similar conclusion holds if $m(t' + \epsilon)$ is a pooled message. Therefore a universally divine equilibrium cannot have any jump discontinuities from or to pooled segments, leaving only the separating equilibrium as a candidate. Finally, in this equilibrium the out-of-equilibrium messages are $m < m^c(\underline{t})$ and $m > m(\bar{t})$; however by applying the same logic as above we see that universal divinity requires $\mu(\underline{t}, m) = 1$ for the former and $\mu(\bar{t}, m) = 1$ for the latter, beliefs which (as noted) do not provide the incentive for any type to defect. Therefore the unique universally divine equilibrium in the continuous-type Spence model is the unique separating sequential equilibrium.

Clearly, while we have shown the existence of a separating equilibrium in the Spence model with continuous types, and shown this to be the unique universally divine equilibrium, we are unable to obtain a closed-form solution to the sender's equilibrium strategy, since the relevant differential equation is non-linear. However in other continuous-type models such an explicit characterization is readily available. Consider the following model of pre-trial bargaining, due to Reinganum and Wilde [68]. Let $t \in T$ denote the damages of a plaintiff (S) in a civil suit, and let m denote the plaintiff's take-it-or-leave-it settlement demand to the defendant (R). The defendant can then either accept the demand, in which case R transfers the amount m to S, or reject, in which case the parties proceed to court. The court then identifies with certainty the level of damages, R transfers t to S, and S and R incur court costs of c_s and c_r, respectively.

Let $r(m)$ denote the probability the defendant accepts a demand of m from the plaintiff; then the expected utility to S from offering m, given type t and strategy $r(\cdot)$ by R, is:

$$U_S(t, m, r) = r(m) \cdot m + (1 - r(m)) \cdot (t - c_s)$$
$$= r(m) \cdot (m - t + c_s) + (t - c_s), \qquad (21)$$

which from Section 2.2 is utility equivalent to

$$\tilde{U}_S(t, m, r) = r(m) \cdot (m - t + c_s). \qquad (22)$$

The defendant's expected utility from accepting a demand of m with probability r, given beliefs λ, is

$$U_R(\lambda, m, r) = -r \cdot m - (1 - r) \cdot (t_\lambda + c_r), \qquad (23)$$

where $t_\lambda \equiv E_\lambda(t)$ is the expected value of the sender's type according to the distribution λ. Therefore R's best response is

$$BR(\lambda, m) = \begin{cases} 1 & \text{if } m < t_\lambda + c_r \\ [0, 1] & \text{if } m = t_\lambda + c_r \\ 0 & \text{if } m > t_\lambda + c_r \end{cases} \qquad (24)$$

As in the Spence model it is 'easily' shown that in any sequential equilibrium $m(t)$ will be weakly increasing, while $r(m(t))$ will be weakly decreasing. In particular, if $m(t)$ is strictly increasing at t, then the probability of acceptance $r(.)$ must be strictly decreasing at $m(t)$. To sustain separation, then, it must be that $r(.)$ is strictly between 0 and 1 at all $m(t)$, except possibly at $m(\underline{t})$, thereby requiring the receiver to be indifferent between accepting and rejecting the equilibrium messages.

Further, since $m(\cdot)$ is assumed to be separating, upon observing $m(t)$ the receiver knows with certainty that the sender's type is t. Thus from eq. (24) if in equilibrium $m(\cdot)$ is separating, it must be that for all $t \in T$ $m(t) = t + c_r$. The receiver's acceptance schedule $r(\cdot)$ then must provide the incentive for the sender to propose $t + c_r$ when his type is t, i.e. if S is of type t $r(.)$ must be such that

$$t + c_r \in \operatorname*{argmax}_m r(m) \cdot (m - t + c_s). \tag{25}$$

Since $r(\cdot)$ will be differentiable for all $m \in (\underline{t} + c_r, \bar{t} + c_r)$, the first-order condition associated with the above optimization program is

$$\frac{\partial r}{\partial m} + r(m) \cdot \frac{1}{m - t + c_s} = 0 \tag{26}$$

Substituting in $m = t + c_r$, we get the following first-order linear differential equation

$$\frac{\partial r}{\partial m} + r(m)/C = 0, \tag{27}$$

where $C = c_s + c_r$. The general solution to eq. (27) is

$$r(m) = k \cdot exp\{- m/C\}, \tag{28}$$

where k is a constant of integration. The boundary condition is

$$r(\underline{t} + c_r) = 1, \tag{29}$$

which follows from a similar argument as in the Spence model; this then determines the value of k. Thus the following constitute the strategies in a separating equilibrium:

$$m(t) = t + c_r \forall t \in T, \tag{30}$$

$$r(m) = \begin{cases} 1 & \text{if } m \le t + c_r \\ exp\{(\underline{t} + c_r - m)/C\} & \text{if } m \in [\underline{t} + c_r, \bar{t} + c_r], \\ 0 & \text{else} \end{cases} \tag{31}$$

As in the Spence model there exist pooling equilibria (for some prior beliefs) as well as equilibria where some types separate while others (locally) pool. Thus the refinement arguments discussed above may be of some use in narrowing the set of predicted behavior. Indeed,

Reinganum and Wilde [68] prove that, as in the Spence model, the unique separating equilibrium is also the unique universally divine equilibrium.[10]

Thus analyzing signaling games with continuous types is not in general any more difficult than with finite types; indeed in some instances it is easier since the analyst can apply simple calculus techniques to solve for the equilibrium strategies. However, as the Spence example shows, an explicit characterization of these strategies may be problematic.

2.6. Costless signaling

In the examples above the message sent by the sender can be thought of as playing a dual role in the decision process, namely a *substantive* role in directly affecting the payoffs of S and R, as well as an *informational* role, in that R is attempting to infer from the choice of message the sender's true type. Hence in certain situations these roles will induce a tension in the sender's decision calculus, in that a message which is preferable on substantive grounds may be less so when the receiver's inference and resulting response are considered.

In some of the models examined below, however, the sender's messages play only an informational role, i.e. the message chosen does not directly affect the players' utilities. In such games, we can write the utility functions without loss of generality as

$$U_i(t, m, r), \; i = U_i(t, r) = S, R. \qquad (32)$$

These games are sometimes known as *costless* signaling games, in that the 'cost' to the players from the sender sending one message relative to any other message is zero. Thus the messages only indirectly affect the players' utilities through the (possibly) different actions induced by the different messages. In addition, it is clear the receiver's decision calculus is identical following every message, up to a specification of R's posterior beliefs. Thus for all messages m, $m' \in M$ and all beliefs $\lambda \in \Delta(T)$, $BR(\lambda, m) = BR(\lambda, m')$.

Another implication of costless signaling is that there can be no intrinsic meaning or interpretation of a message, since if there exists an

---

[10] However, not all continuous-type signaling games have separating equilibria; cf. the model of Banks [13] described in Section 3.3 below.

equilibrium (s, r, μ) where some types T_1 to send m' and other types T_2 send m'', then there will also exist an equilibrium $(\tilde{s}, \tilde{r}, \tilde{\mu})$ where types T_1 to send m'' and T_2 send m'. This follows since $\mu(m') = \tilde{\mu}(m'')$ and $\mu(m'') = \tilde{\mu}(m')$, which implies $BR(\mu, m') = BR(\tilde{\mu}, m'')$ and $BR(\mu, m'')$ $= BR(\tilde{\mu}, m')$, so that defining $\tilde{r}(m'') = r(m')$ and $\tilde{r}(m') = r(m'')$ gives both a best response by $\Re$ to $\tilde{s}$ and provides the appropriate incentives for types in T_1 and T_2. Thus there cannot be any meaningful description about what messages are sent in equilibrium; the only relevant feature of the sender's strategy is *how much* information is being revealed.

Unfortunately, still another implication of costless signaling games is that there always exist pooling equilibria regardless of the structure of payoffs or the prior beliefs. To see this, consider the following behavior: $s^*(m', t) = 1$, $\forall t \in T$, $r^*(m) = BR(p, m)$, $\forall m \in M$, and $\mu^*(t, m) = p(t) \forall m \in M$. Thus R's posterior belief following any message is simply the prior belief, implying R can take the same action following any message. Given this response the sender is indifferent between all possible messages, since they all lead to the same response. Since this holds for all types, then, all types pooling on the message m' is optimal. Hence R believing that no information is ever transmitted through the messages, and hence always believing the prior, is always part of an equilibrium regardless of the payoff structure of the game. Indeed, since m' is arbitrary, there exists as many pooling equilibria as there are messages. Such behavior can be seen as a particular form of 'babbling' equilibrium, where for all $m \in M$ $s^*(m; t) = s^*(m; t')$ for all $t, t' \in T$, implying for all equilibrium messages $\mu^*(t; m) = p(t)$. In such an equilibrium, even though S sends potentially all of the messages with positive probability, these probabilities are the same for all types, implying no 'useful' information is transmitted to the receiver.

At the other extreme with respect to informativeness are separating equilibria, where in Section 4 below we show how such equilibria can exist in costless signaling games. In such games there will exist equilibria that are completely uninformative (i.e. babbling), as well as those that are completely informative (i.e. separating). These games typically assume the sets T, M, A, are finite; indeed, Crawford and Sobel [28] show that with continuous sets such separation becomes problematic, implying that the most informative equilibria will involve some amounts of pooling. Let $T = [\underline{t}, \overline{t}] \subset \mathbb{R}$, $M = A = \mathbb{R}$, and assume U_S and U_R are twice continuously differentiable, where for each $i = S$, R, $\partial U_i(t, r)/\partial r = 0$ for some r and $\partial^2 U_i/\partial r^2 < 0$, so that U_i has a unique maximum in r for each t. Further assume $\partial^2 U_i / \partial r \partial t > 0$, so that the maximizing value of r is a strictly increasing function of t. Define $\rho_i(t) \equiv \text{argmax } U_i(t, r)$, $i = S$, R, as the complete information U_i – maximizing response by the receiver; by the above assumptions these are well-defined and continuous in t. Then Crawford and Sobel [28] show that if $\rho_s(t) \neq \rho_r(t) \forall t \in T$, i.e. the preferences of the players differ, separating equilibria cannot occur. In fact, *all* of the equilibria are equivalent to 'partition' equilibria of the following form: let $t_1 = \underline{t}$, $t_n = \overline{t}$, and $\forall j \in \{2, \ldots, n - 1\} t_j$ is such that $t_{j-1} < t_j < t_{j+1}$, and let $\{m_1, \ldots, m_n\}$ be a set of distinct messages from M. In equilibrium, then, $s^*(m_j, t) > 0$ only if $t \in [t_j, t_{j+1})$. Thus if R observes the messages m_j he can infer that t is in the set $[t_j, t_{j+1})$, and updates the prior belief accordingly. Clearly if $n = 1$ we have pooling equilibria; for $n > 2$, then, some information is being revealed through the equilibrium messages. In addition, there exists a finite bound on n, the number of elements in the partition, where this bound is a function of the similarity of the players' preferences: the closer are S and R's preferred alternatives, the higher is the bound on the number of partitions, and hence the more informative is the most informative equilibria. Alternatively, if the preferences of S and R are sufficiently diverse, the bound is equal to 1; only pooling equilibria can be sustained.

Thus depending on the diversity of the players' preferences there may exist equilibria with varying degrees of informativeness, raising again the issue of selecting among these as the behavioral or qualitative prediction from the model. However it is immediate that the equilibrium refinements discussed in Section 2.4 above can have no impact in costless signaling games. To see this, suppose t sends m' and R responds with a'; then for any unsent message m there exists a belief which gives a' as a best response, since $BR(m') = BR(m)$. Given this response t is indifferent between sending m and m', and no type strictly prefers to send m relative to their equilibrium payoff; otherwise such a type would have been better off sending m' originally. But since this holds for all types and all out-of-equilibrium messages, there do not exist responses by R which effectively discriminate among the types. Therefore any type is as likely as any other to defect to a previously unsent message.

Although there has been some work on constructing refinements for costless signaling games, most notably Farrell [33], the more common approach has been to select out those equilibria which are most informative. One motivation for this selection concerns simply the issue of how much information can possibly be transmitted in the model in question; in particular, if in the Crawford and Sobel [28] model $n = 1$, then the situation is such that no useful information can be transmitted from the sender to the receiver. Alternatively, Crawford and Sobel [28] show in their general model that, from an *ex ante* perspective (i.e. prior to S realizing her type) both the receiver as well as the sender prefer equilibria with larger numbers of partitions. Thus an efficiency argument can also provide a justification for examining only the most informative equilibria. This result also justifies the selection when the relevant comparison is between the expected utilities in certain costless versus 'costly' signaling games: if e.g. an equilibrium with costly signaling is Pareto-preferred to the most informative equilibria in the costless signaling game, then it follows that it is preferred to *all* equilibria with costless signaling. In general then the focus in costless signaling games will be on the most informative equilibria as the behavioral prediction.

2.7. Discussion

In this section we have examined the basic model of information signaling which underlies the analysis in the papers to follow. In each of these we will attempt to state the model in notation and language analogous to that used above. However we will refrain from laboriously working through the applications of sequential equilibrium (and possibly its refinements) in each of the models, and instead restrict most of our attention to the qualitative features of the equilibria themselves. At times this will be most efficiently pursued by simply examining the equilibrium path of play, i.e. the message sent $m^*(t)$ as well as the responses induced by those messages $r^*(m^*(t)) \equiv r^*(t)$, and ignoring or succinctly summarizing out-of-equilibrium behavior. In this way we can focus on the principal substantive arguments generated by the models, such as the ability of the sender to transmit information to the receiver through the chosen message strategy, and the differential behavior by the players in the presence of complete versus incomplete information concerning relevant decision parameters. Yet at times it will be useful to consider why certain strategies do or do not constitute equilibrium behavior. It is hoped that such a task is made easier by the preceding examples and analyses.

3. AGENDA CONTROL

3.1. Introduction

The literature on agenda control generally concerns a social decision problem wherein one participant is differentially advantaged relative to others in their ability to influence the outcome. One of the classic instances of such an arrangement is the use of closed or restrictive rules in legislative decision-making (cf. Denzau and Mackay [30]) under which a particular subset of a collective is able to determine the set of alternatives from which the collective can select an outcome. Consider a one-dimensional policy space $X \subset \mathbb{R}$ from which two players, labelled the committee and the floor, select a final outcome from X, and where the floor is decisive in any choice of outcomes. Assume the floor and the committee have single-peaked symmetric preferences over X, with the floor's ideal outcome equal to $x = 0$ and the committee's equal to $x_c > 0$. Under a *closed rule* the committee is permitted to make a 'take-it-or-leave-it' proposal to the floor, ie. if the committee proposes x, then the floor's choice is either to accept or reject x, where rejection implies the outcome is equal to the 'status quo' outcome x_0.

The unique equilibrium prediction with complete information is then easily characterized as a function of the parameter x_0: if $|x_0| \geq x_c$ the committee proposes $x = x_c$, which the floor subsequently accepts, since the committee's ideal outcome is preferred by the floor to the status quo; if $x_0 \in (-x_c, 0)$ the committee proposes $-x_0$, which is the outcome closest to x_c that is acceptable to the floor, and the floor accepts; finally if $x_0 \in [0, x_c)$ the committee makes a proposal which the floor rejects, generating a final outcome of x_0. Therefore as long as the status quo outcome x_0 is inefficient relative to the preferences of the floor and committee, i.e. $x_0 \notin [0, x_c)$ the committee can move the final outcome in its preferred direction through its control of the 'agenda' faced by the floor. Under the *open rule*, on the other hand, the assumption is that the floor can propose any alternative in response to the committee's proposal, in essense eliminating any agenda control by the committee. Thus given the environment above the proposal by the committee has no impact on the outcome under the open rule; the floor simply implements its ideal outcome $x = 0$. Thus the floor always prefers the open rule to the closed rule, while the opposite is true for the committee.

An important substantive question then concerns explaining the use of the closed rule in Congress, given that in general the floor is the more authoritative body and hence has control over the choice of rules. Gilligan and Krehbiel [36], [37] provide an explanation by relaxing the assumption of complete information, analyzing models in which the committee possesses an informational advantage *vis-à-vis* the floor. These models dovetail nicely with the 'classic' literature on committees in legislatures, wherein committees exist precisely because of the presence of informational asymmetries (cf. Cooper [27]). The presence of these asymmetries implies that the ability of the committee to make 'better' decisions may outweigh the bias in the decisions in favor of the committee's ideal outcome, a logic which Gilligan and Krehbiel address. In Gilligan and Krehbiel [36] the committee is modeled as a unitary actor, while in Gilligan and Krehbiel [37] there are two committee members possessing the same information but with divergent preferences as well as possibly differential access to the agenda.[11]

Romer and Rosenthal [71], [72] analyze the same basic model of complete information agenda control outlined above but in a somewhat different context. In their situation the 'agenda setter' is not a committee but is rather a budget-maximizing bureaucrat who proposes a budget to his constituents; these constituents can then either accept the proposed budget or reject and implement the status quo budget. The principal difference in the Romer-Rosenthal model from that above is that the ideal outcome for the agenda setter is infinite, $x_c = \infty$. If we think of $x = 0$ as the ideal outcome of the 'median' constituent, where majority rule is required for implementation, the complete information equilibrium outcome is simply x_0 if $x_0 \geq 0$ and $-x_0$ if $x_0 < 0$. In particular, for status quo outcomes less than the median constituent's ideal outcome there exists a negative relationship between the status quo and the final (equilibrium) outcome: lower status quos generate higher outcomes, so the lower is the status quo budget of the bureaucrat the higher the budget the bureaucrat can extract from the constituents.

Banks [13] generalizes the Romer–Rosenthal model by assuming only the bureaucrat is aware of the precise value of the status quo

---

[11] In addition, Gilligan and Krehbiel [38] examine a model where the rule is selected by the floor after the committee's proposal.

outcome, and then examines whether this negative relationship persists with incomplete information. Here the key issue concerns the ability of the agenda setter to signal the true status quo through the choice of proposal. An additional question is whether the agenda setter remains so dramatically advantaged relative to the constituents, again attempting to address the issue of the rational presence of agenda control. Banks [17] then extends this model by further assuming the preferences of the median constituent are not known with certainty by the agenda setter, and finds an opposite result concerning the informativeness of the setter's strategy.

A final example of models of agenda control include those studying the interaction between legislatures and bureaucrats or agencies in the determination of an agency's budget, where the agency is a producer of goods valued by the legislature, which in turn 'oversees' the behavior of the agency. The classic model of Niskanen [63] assumes the agency has complete control over deciding on its own output level and hence its own budget, and where the agency prefers higher budgets than does the legislature. Therefore the general prediction is for overproduction relative to that preferred by the legislature, again raising the issue of why such a bias can persist given the legislature's presumed superior status.

As with the models of committees, Niskanen assumes that the reason for this strategic asymmetry is that there exists an informational asymmetry between the agency and the legislature, implying that granting the agency agenda control may be optimal. Banks [12] examines this claim in a model where the legislature has an inelastic demand for one unit of the agency's services and where the agency knows the cost of its services while the legislature does not.[12] Hence the key question is not the relative overproduction by the agency but rather the ability of the agency to extract higher budgets from the legislature. Procedures analogous to the closed and open rules discussed above are analyzed, where the strategic opportunities of the legislature are augmented by assuming that, in its oversight role, the legislature has the ability to 'audit' the agency at a cost and subsequently determine the actual cost of the agency's services.[13] As with the work of Gilligan

---

[12] See Banks [16] for the model with a linear demand schedule.

[13] Bendor, Taylor, and Van Gaalen [20] examine a similar model in a principal-agent framework.

and Krehbiel [36], Banks [12] derives the induced preferences of the players over the various procedures to determine the rationality of granting the agency an advantageous strategic role in the determination of its own budget.

3.2. Restrictive rules in legislatures

The model of Gilligan and Krehbiel [36] assumes the committee plays the role of the sender S, with the floor being the receiver R. The committee's type is drawn from $T = [0, 1]$ according to the density $f(\cdot)$, where $f(\cdot)$ is assumed to be uniform. The space of outcomes is $X = \mathbb{R}$, where the players' preferences over X are represented by the functions $u_S(x) = -(x - x_s)^2$, $x_s > 0$, and $u_R(x) = -x^2$. Thus S and R have quadratic preferences over X, with the floor's ideal point being $x = 0$ and the committee's $x = x_s$.

Under the closed rule the strategy sets are as follows: $M = \mathbb{R}$, so the committee can propose any outcome, and $A = \{a_1, a_2\}$, where a_1 denotes acceptance of the proposal m, and a_2 denotes rejection; let $r(m)$ be the probability that R accepts a proposal of $m \in M$.[14] The preferences of S and R over $T \times M \times A$ are then

$$U_S(t, m, r) = -r\cdot(m + t - x_s)^2 - (1 - r)\cdot(x_0 + t - x_s)^2, \qquad (33)$$

$$U_R(t, m, r) = -r\cdot(m + t)^2 - (1 - r)\cdot(x_0 + t)^2, \qquad (34)$$

where x_0 is the status quo outcome; assume that $x_0 < 0$. The interpretation of the committee's type t is as a shift parameter: given that the outcome chosen by S and R is x, the *consequence* of that choice is not x but rather $x + t$. In this sense then the committee possesses an informational advantage relative to the floor, since it knows precisely the consequences associated with any particular outcome. Alternatively, we can think of the floor's *induced* ideal point on X as $-t$, and the committee's as $x_s - t$, where now the committee knows with certainty the induced preferences of S and R over X.

The best response correspondence of R is as follows: given beliefs λ, if R accepts m his expected utility is equal to $U_R(\lambda, m, a_1) = -\int_T (m + t)^2\cdot\lambda(t)dt = -(m + t_\lambda)^2 - \sigma_\lambda^2$, where t_λ is the mean and σ_λ^2 the

---

[14] Gilligan and Krehbiel [36] restrict attention to pure strategies for the floor.

variance associated with the density λ. Similarly if R rejects m his expected utility is $U_R(\lambda, m, a_2) = -(x_0 + t_\lambda)^2 - \sigma_\lambda^2$. Thus

$$BR(\lambda, m) = \begin{cases} 1 & < \\ [0, 1] \text{ if } d(m, t_\lambda) = d(x_0, t_\lambda); & \\ 0 & > \end{cases} \qquad (35)$$

i.e. R's optimal response to any message will simply be a function of which is closer, m or x_0, to the mean value of the shift parameter t_λ.[15]

For the sender the preferences characterized by $U_S(t, m, r)$ are utility equivalent to

$$\begin{aligned} \tilde{U}_S(t, m, r) &\equiv U_S(t, m, r) + (x_0 + t - x_z)^2 \\ &= -r \cdot [(m + t - x_s)^2 - (x_0 + t - x_s)^2] \\ &= r \cdot (x_0 - m) \cdot [m + x_0 + 2(t - x_s)]. \end{aligned} \qquad (36)$$

Given this expression it is easily shown by incentive compatibility[16] that in any equilibrium $m^*(t)$ is monotone decreasing on the set of types $T^+ = \{t \in T: r^*(m^*(t)) > 0\}$. Thus higher types make (weakly) lower proposals in equilibrium. In addition, incentive compatibility implies that if $t > t'$ and $t, t' \in T^+$, (so $m^*(t) \leq m^*(t')$), and $m^*(t) > x_0$, then $r^*(t) \geq r^*(t')$, i.e. higher types have their equilibrium proposals accepted with (weakly) higher probability, whereas if $m^*(t') < x_0, r^*(t) \leq r^*(t')$.

Before examining the equilibrium that Gilligan and Krehbiel [36] consider, it is informative to understand why there does *not* exist a separating equilibrium where $r^*(t) > 0$ for all $t \in T$. First note that S has a weakly dominant strategy if $t = x_s - x_0$ of proposing $m = x_0$, since regardless of whether this proposal is accepted or rejected S receives his highest possible utility. Therefore if $r^*(x_s - x_0) > 0$ then it must be that $m^*(x_s - x_0) = x_0$. Now suppose $t = -x_0$ separates and $r^*(t) > 0$. Then the payoff to R from accepting $m^*(-x_0)$ must be at least as great as rejecting it, yet rejection gives R (by separation) his highest payoff. Thus R would accept only if $m^*(-x_0)$ makes R indifferent, implying $m^*(-x_0) = x_0$. But this would also have to be $m^*(x_s - x_0)$, implying there is no separating equilibrium where all types' proposals are accepted with positive probability.

The equilibrium on which Gilligan Krehbiel [36] focus under the

---

[15] This follows since the floor's induced ideal point given beliefs λ is simply t_λ.
[16] See Section 2.5.

closed rule has the following path: if $t \in [0, -3x_s - x_0] \cup [x_s - x_0, 1] \equiv$ T_1, then $m^*(t) = x_s - t$ and $r^*(t) = 1$, so that the committee separates in its proposal, and (given the inferred value of t) the floor strictly prefers to accept rather than reject the proposal. Further, the committee receives its highest possible payoff, $U_S^*(t) = 0$. If $t \in [-3x_s - x_0, -x_s - x_0] \equiv T_2$, then $m^*(t) = 4x_s + x_0$ and $r^*(t) = 1$, so that these types pool and have the proposal accepted, while if $t \in (-x_s - x_0, x_s - x_0] \equiv T_3$ then $m^*(t) \in (x_0, x_0 + 4x_s)$ and $r^*(t) = 0$, i.e. these types pool and have the proposal rejected. Thus for extreme values of the shift parameter t the committee is able to both separate and generate their maximum payoff, while more moderate types are unable to perform either of these functions.

Note how the behavior in the separating segments differs from that in the Reinganum–Wilde [68] example in Section 2.5. In the latter the receiver's response strategy had to provide the incentive for the sender not to send higher messages, where such messages were preferable for the sender given a fixed response by R. Such incentives could only be generated by the receiver being indifferent between his two possible actions, implying R could mix in his response to the equilibrium messages and choose to adopt an acceptance schedule that provided the correct incentives. In the current model however no such incentive role is needed. Given a finite ideal point the committee does not necessarily prefer higher outcomes to lower so that, since each type is receiving his highest possible payoff (an outcome not possible in the earlier example), the fact that R's response strategy upon observing these equilibrium messages is 'flat' is not inconsistent with equilibrium behavior. Indeed, given their focus on pure strategy responses by the receiver, it is evident that separation only occurs in Gilligan and Krehbiel [36] because of the finiteness of the sender's (induced) ideal point; if S's utility over outcomes in $\mathbb{R}$ was strictly increasing, no separation could occur in pure strategies.

In addition, note that some types are having their equilibrium proposal rejected by the floor, which again differs from the previous example. The logic behind this certain rejection being an equilibrium phenomenon is the fact that these types receive a relatively high payoff (and, as noted above for $t = x_s - x_0$ the highest possible payoff) from simply allowing the status quo to be the outcome. A continuity argument then shows that if $r^*(x_s - x_0) = 0$ there will exist an interval of types, including $x_s - x_0$, where $r^*(t) = 0$.

Under the open rule the floor has the ability to implement any outcome in X, including the status quo x_0, so that $A = X$. Hence the proposal $m \in M$ by the committee plays a purely informational role in the process, i.e. the game is one with costless signaling. Let $a(m) \in X$ be the outcome selected by the floor following a proposal of m by the committee; then

$$U_S(t, m, a) = -(a + t - x_s)^2, \tag{37}$$

$$U_R(t, m, a) = -(a + t)^2. \tag{38}$$

The best response correspondence is then

$$BR(\lambda, m) = \operatorname*{argmax}_{a \in A} \int -(a + t)^2 \cdot \lambda(t) dt,$$

$$= \operatorname*{argmax}_{a \in A} -(a + t_\lambda)^2 - \sigma_\lambda^2, \tag{39}$$

implying $BR(\lambda, m) = -t_\lambda$; the floor implements its induced ideal point.

Since the game under the open rule is one with costless signaling, we know from Section 2.6 that there will exist completely uninformative pooling equilibria at all $m \in M$, and in general an infinite number of babbling equilibria. In addition, since this is a game with continuous types and the players' preferences satisfy the assumptions of Crawford and Sobel [28], and differ, i.e. $x_s > 0$, there will not exist a separating equilibrium. The equilibrium path which Gilligan and Krehbiel [36] analyze under the open rule is a semi-pooling strategy by S similar to the partition equilibrium in Section 2.6 in which the 'maximum' amount of information can be inferred. Let $t_0 = 0$, $t_N = 1$, where N is the largest integer satisfying $|2N \cdot (1 - N) \cdot x_s| < 1$, and define t_i, $1 < i < N$ by

$$t_i = t_1 \cdot i + 2 \cdot i \cdot (1 - i) \cdot x_s; \tag{40}$$

thus the equilibria will be parameterized by the choice of t_1. Then the class of equilibrium strategies for S is

$$m^*(t) \in [x_s - t_{i+1}, x_s - t_i), \ t \in [t_i, t_{i+1}). \tag{41}$$

Since $f(\cdot)$ is uniform R's equilibrium response to observing $m^*(t)$ is $a^* = -(t_{i+1} - t_i)/2$, since R's updated belief about t is such that the mean value is $t_\mu = (t_{i+1} - t_i)/2$. For the committee's strategy to be optimal, then, it is sufficient to show that for all $i = 1, \ldots, N$, $t = t_i$ is indifferent between proposing $m^*(t_i - \epsilon)$ and $m^*(t_i + \epsilon)$. Since the t_is are increasing, this is true if and only if

$$t_{i+1} = 2t_i - t_{i-1} - 4x_s, \tag{42}$$

which is a second-order difference equation whose solution is given in eq. (40) above. Therefore the equilibria under the open rule have N distinct proposals offered in equilibrium, implying a partition of T into N different subintervals governing the behavior of the committee. In equilibrium the floor will be able to infer the shift parameter t up to an identification of one of the subintervals, but no further. Hence some information is being transmitted from the committee to the floor, but not all of the available information.

As noted above, the central concern of Gilligan and Krehbiel [36] is the issue of rationalizing the prevalence of closed or restrictive rules given the floor's presumed ability to dictate such a choice. With complete information it is clear that granting such a strategic advantage to the committee when the preferences of the floor and committee diverge is never in the floor's interests. On the other hand with incomplete information Gilligan and Krehbiel [36] show the following: there exists a bound $x^* > 0$ such that if $x_s \leq x^*$ then the floor prefers the *ex ante* expected utility generated by the equilibrium under the closed rule to that generated under the open rule.[17] Therefore if the preferences of the committee and floor are not too diverse, the floor actually prefers to relinquish its proposal-making ability to the committee. The key to this result is the following: under both the open and closed rules the expected equilibrium utility of the floor is decreasing in x_s, so that as their preferences become less diverse the floor is better off under either rule. For the open rule this is true since, as discussed in Section 2.6, the more homogeneous the preferences the greater is the committee's ability to transmit information, leading to a more informed decision by the floor. Under the closed rule the set of types that separate and subsequently implement their induced ideal outcome is itself increasing as x_s decreases, and as x_s decreases the committee's ideal outcome becomes more favorable from the floor's perspective. Now in selecting the closed over open rule the floor faces a distributional loss, due to the committee being able to bias the resulting outcome in its favor, as well as an informational gain, due to the

---

[17] Recall the equilibrium ranking by R in terms of expected payoffs in Section 2.6.

increased amount of information transmitted and the assumed risk aversion of the floor. Gilligan and Krehbiel show that as x_s decreases this distributional loss tends to be outweighed by the informational gains, implying the closed rule is preferable. On the other hand as x_s increases the distributional loss tend to dominate, implying the open rule is preferable.

Thus Gilligan and Krehbiel [36] show that instituting a closed rule in a legislative setting, thereby conferring on the relevant committees a degree of agenda control, can be a rational response to the presence of informational asymmetries in the decision making process. The ability of the committee to implement informed yet biased outcomes will in some circumstances be preferable for the floor to itself implementing less biased yet less informed decisions.

Gilligan and Krehbiel [37] extend their earlier model by assuming that the behavior of the committee is not characterized by a single member, but rather by two, where both of these committee members have the same level of 'expertise' i.e. they both are cognizant of the shift parameter t, and this is common knowledge. Let S_1, S_2 represent these two 'senders', who simultaneously select messages from M_1, M_2, respectively, $M_1 = M_2 = \mathbb{R}$, where now a response by the receiver is a function $r: M_1 \times M_2 \to \Delta(A)$, so that $a(m_1, m_2)$ is an action induced by the message pair (m_1, m_2). The preferences of R over outcomes in X are as before, namely quadratic on $\mathbb{R}$ about zero, while S_i's are quadratic about x_i; assume $x_1 > 0$ and $x_2 = -x_1$, so the preferences of the committee members are diametrically opposed relatively to movements away from the floor's ideal outcome.

With the above environment, Gilligan and Krehbiel [37] analyze three different rules, where each rule defines the relevant set of actions for the floor: 1) the open rule, where $A = \mathbb{R}$, so that each committee member proposes an alternative from $\mathbb{R}$ and the floor selects the final outcome from $\mathbb{R}$; 2) the modified rule, where $A = \{a_1, a_2, a_0\}$ and action a_i denotes acceptance of proposal m_i, $i = 1, 2$, and a_0 denotes rejection of both proposals and the subsequent implementation of the status quo x_0; and 3) the closed rule, where $A = \{a_1, a_0\}$, so the proposal by S_2 is a form of costless signaling. The relevant questions then concern the informativeness of the equilibrium strategies and the subsequent distribution of payoffs in the presence of conflicting incentives on the part of the informed players.

Under the open rule, Gilligan and Krehbiel [37] show that, in contrast to their earlier model, it is possible to sustain separation even though both messages are costless. In the equilibrium they analyze, if $t < 1/2 - 2x_1$ or $t > 1/2 + 2x_1$, $m_1^*(t) = x_1 - t$ and $m_2^*(t) = -x_2 - t$, and $a(m^*(t)) = m_1^*(t) - t$. Thus for extreme values of t, both senders separate in their message strategy, implying that the floor responds with its complete information optimal response equal to its induced ideal point $-t$. For $t \in [1/2 - 2x_1, 1/2 + 2x_1]$, on the other hand, both senders pool and the floor selects $-1/2$, the negative of the *ex ante* expected value of t.[18] The floor provides the incentive for the senders to separate by adopting the response equal to $m_1^* - 1/2$ if $m_1^* - m_2^* = 2x_1$, and responding with $-1/2$ otherwise; therefore the choice for (say) S_1, given the stratgegy m_2^*, is between the floor's induced ideal point $-t$ and the floor's *ex ante* expected ideal point $-1/2$. For extreme values of t the former is preferred by S_1 to the latter. The key to this being an equilibrium is the receiver's ability to 'punish' the senders when their messages fail to coincide by selecting $-1/2$ even when one of the senders is sending a message which is consistent with the separating region of the equilibrium strategy m^*.

Under the modified rule Gilligan and Krehbiel [37] identify the following equilibrium path: if $t > 2x_1 - x_0$ then $m_1^*(t) = -t$, $m_2^*(t) = -x_1 - t$, and $a(m^*(t)) = a_1$, so that both senders separate, and S_1 proposes the floor's induced complete information ideal point, which the floor subsequently accepts; if $t < -2x_1 - x_0$ then $m_1^*(t) = x_1 - t$, $m_2^*(t) = -t$, and $a(m^*(t)) = a_2$, so that now S_2 proposes the floor's induced ideal point, which the floor accepts; and if $t \in [-2x_1 - x_0, 2x_1 - x_0]$ the senders pool and the floor selects the status quo.

Note that if $x_0 = -1/2$ the equilibrium outcomes under the open and modified rules are identical; in particular, the separating and pooling regions coincide, with the separating regions generating the floor's complete information induced ideal outcome and the pooling regions generating the floor's *ex ante* expected induced ideal outcome. Therefore the informational and distributional effects of the rules coincide as well, and as Gilligan and Krehbiel [37] note, 'a restrictive rule for a heterogeneous committee is neither a distributional asset to the committee (whose members exercise no power in equilibrium) nor an informational asset to the [floor] (whose inferences are no more precise than under the open rule).'

---

[18] Recall that the prior $f(\cdot)$ is assumed to be uniform.

Under the closed rule, where S_2's message is 'costless', the equilibrium path is as follows: if $t \leq -3x_1 - x_0$ or $t \geq x_1 - x_0$, $m_1^*(t) = x_1 - t$, $m_2^*(t) = t$, and $a(m^*(t)) = a_1$, so S_1 separates and offers his induced ideal outcome, which the floor accepts; if $t \in (-3x_1 - x_0, -x_1 - x_0)$ $m_1^*(t) = -2(x_1 + t) - x_0$, $m_2^*(t) = t$, and $a(m^*(t)) = a_1$, so S_1 separates and offers an alternative which is preferred by the floor to S_1's ideal outcome and to the status quo, and the floor accepts; and if $t \in (-x_1 - x_0, x_1 - x_0)$ both senders pool and $a(m^*(t)) = a_0$. In sum, then, as with the closed rule with a homogeneous committee, for extreme values of t, S_1 is able to implement his induced ideal outcome, while for moderate values S_1 implements an outcome more favorable to the floor. In particular, the ability of S_2 to send a costless message to the floor mitigates the ability of S_1 to implement his ideal outcome by shrinking the set of such separating types, as well as forcing some moderate types to separate to an intermediate outcome. Thus relative to the open and modified rules, the closed rule generates informational gains for the floor, in that the separating regions are larger, as well as distributional losses, in that the equilibrium outcomes are at times biased in favor of S_1.

Under the closed rule the interpretation of S_2's message is as a 'speech' concerning the value of the parameter t, whereas under the open rule the interpretation of both senders' messages are as proposals which the floor can subsequently amend. However the key is that in both instances the message by S_2 is costless, and since there is no unique literal meaning to these messages,[19] one way we can scale these three rules is by *how many* senders' signals are costless. Thus under the open rule both senders engage in costless signaling, under the closed rule, S_2 does but S_1 does not (since his proposal may be accepted), and under the modified rule neither senders' message is costless (either proposal might be accepted). Given this scaling, we observe a non-monotonicity in the associated equilibrium outcomes: when both senders engage in costless signaling or when neither do the outcomes are the same, whereas when only one sender's signal is costless the behavior differs, and the floor experiences informational gains and distributional losses relative to the other rules. In particular, the informativeness of the senders' strategies is maximized when exactly one of the senders' signals is costless.

---

[19] See the discussion in Section 2.6.

In comparing the models with homogeneous versus heterogeneous committees, Gilligan and Krehbiel [37] identify the following result: from an informational standpoint the closed rule equilibrium with a homogeneous committee is equivalent to the open or modified rule equilibrium with a heterogeneous committee. Therefore 'restrictive rules and heterogeneous committees appear to be informational substitutes.' Recalling that with a homogeneous committee the floor prefers *ex ante* the closed rule to the open when the former's informational gains outweigh its distributional losses, it is clear then that the floor can realize these informational gains *without* the associated distributional losses through a decision process whereby informed committee members with conflicting incentives are both given the ability to propose alternatives to the floor. In particular, if we imagine the floor as both the selector of rules and the designer of committees, we would expect the optimal committee structure to include heterogeneous committees along with open or modified rules.

3.3. The monopoly agenda setter model

Banks [13] extends the Romer–Rosenthal [71], [72] model of monopoly agenda control to an environment where only the setter knows the value of the status quo. As in the model of Gilligan and Krehbiel [36] the outcome space is one-dimensional, $X = \mathbb{R}$, where the preferences of the sender over X are represented by a continuously differentiable, strictly increasing, concave function $u_S(\cdot)$, and we assume the receiver's preferences on X are quadratic about zero: $u_R(x) = -x^2$. Let $T = [\underline{t}, \overline{t}]$, where $\underline{t} < 0 < \overline{t}$, with density $f(\cdot)$; thus if the sender's type is t then the status quo outcome will simply be equal to t. The sender can propose any alternative in X, $M = \mathbb{R}$, and the receiver can either accept, a_1, or reject, a_2; let $r(m) = r(a_1, m)$ denote the probability R accepts m.

The players' preferences over $T \times M \times A$ are thus

$$U_i(t, m, r) = r \cdot u_i(m) + (1 - r) \cdot u_i(t), \quad i = S, R. \qquad (43)$$

Since $U_R(\lambda, m, r) = -r \cdot m^2 - (1 - r) \cdot (t_\lambda^2 + \sigma_\lambda^2)$, R's best response correspondence is

$$BR(\lambda, m) = \begin{cases} 1 & < \\ [0, 1] \text{ if } m^2 & = \ t_\lambda^2 + \sigma_\lambda^2. \\ 0 & > \end{cases} \qquad (44)$$

Before characterizing the equilibrium behavior of the model, it is important to note that the assumption of a single voter is without loss of generality if all voters possess quadratic utility functions. Suppose the model consisted of n voters, n odd, where the ideal points of all voters differ. Then as discussed in Section 2.2 in any sequential equilibrium all voters will possess the same beliefs in and out of equilibrium. The assumption of quadratic utilities then implies that for any message m and (common) belief λ there will exist $x(\lambda, m) \in \mathbb{R}$ defined by

$$x = (t_\lambda + m)/2 + \sigma_\lambda^2/[2(t_\lambda - m)] \qquad (45)$$

such that all voters with ideal points less than $x(\lambda, m)$ receive a higher expected utility if m is rejected, while for those with ideal points greater than $x(\lambda, m)$ the opposite is true. Thus if all voters adopt their weakly dominant strategy of voting for their preferred outcome, observing the median voter's decision will be sufficient to determine the majority decision. Hence we can think of R in this model as this median voter in the electorate.

Recall that with complete information the equilibrium is as follows: if $t < 0$ then $m^*(t) = -t$, and $r^*(t) = 1$: if the status quo is less than R's ideal point S proposes the outcome greater than zero which makes R indifferent between accepting and rejecting, and in equilibrium R accepts with probability 1. In particular, there exists a negative relationship between the value of the status quo and the sender's proposal, which in turn is equal to the final outcome. If $t \geq 0$ then $r^*(t) = 0$ and the equilibrium proposal is indeterminate; all that is required is that R rejects the proposal.

With incomplete information about the value of t, Banks [13] first shows that in any equilibrium $m^*(t)$ will be monotone increasing on $[\underline{t}, 0)$, thereby generating an opposite result from the complete information environment; again this monotonicity result follows from incentive compatibility. Second, Banks [13] shows, as in the Gilligan and Krehbiel [36] model, that there does not exist a separating equilibria where $r^*(t) > 0$ for all $t \in T$. In the current model this result holds because of the negative relationship between the expected status quo (for $t_\lambda < 0$) and the willingness of the receiver to accept proposals greater than zero: if $t, t' \in T$ separate, where $t < t' < 0$, and $1 > r^*(t)$, $r^*(t') > 0$, then it must be that (by m^* increasing) $m^*(t') \leq -(t')^2$ and $m^*(t) < -t^2$. But then if R is indifferent upon observing $m^*(t')$, by eq. (44) R will strictly prefer to accept $m^*(t)$, thereby eliminating the ability of R to randomize and subsequently provide the incentive for S to separate. Note how this contrasts with the Reinganum–Wilde [68] model, where such randomization is possible.

Banks [13] then shows that all universally divine equilibria have the following form: $m^*(t) = m \; \forall \; t < m$, $r^*(t) = 1$ if $t < m$ and $r^*(t) = 0$ if $t \geq m$, where m is in the interval $[0, m^+]$ and $m^+ > 0$ is a function of the prior belief $f(\cdot)$. Thus in equilibrium all types $t < 0$ as well as possibly some types $t > 0$ pool together in a proposal which R accepts; the remaining types make proposals which R rejects, so that exactly one proposal is accepted to equilibrium.[20] Therefore separation is not possible in the model, and the information revealed by an equilibrium proposal m^* which is subsequently accepted is simply that t is less than m^*.

Therefore we see that in equilibrium S is not able to differentiate in its behavior and signal to R the precise nature of its information. Clearly for t sufficiently close to $\underline{t}$ such an inability is a hindrance relative to the complete information model, where such types are able to extract substantial gains from R. Alternatively, some types greater than zero actually prefer the incomplete information environment, in that they now have the ability to mimic the behavior of lower types sufficiently to have R accept proposals greater than those occurring if the true status quo were known. Hence the relationship between the status quo and the final outcome changes dramatically when going from complete to incomplete information.

On the other hand, Banks [13] also shows that, from an *ex ante* perspective, there remains something akin to the negative relationship between status quo and final outcome seen with complete information. As noted above m^+, the highest equilibrium proposal accepted, is a function of the prior belief $f(\cdot)$. Suppose $f(\cdot)$ is such that $t_f < 0$ and $|t_f| > \bar{t}$, so according to the prior the expected status quo is less than R's ideal point and in absolute value terms is greater than the highest possible type. Then as the *ex ante* expected status quo decreases the highest acceptable equilibrium proposal increases, $\partial m^+ / \partial t_f < 0$. Therefore, if we select m^+ as our prediction, we get an analogous negative relationship when we consider the *expected* status quo rather than the actual status quo.

---

[20] In any sequential equilibria there are at most two proposals that are accepted with positive probability; from this set then universal divinity selects those with exactly one accepted proposal.

The result that very little information is revealed in equilibrium is somewhat surprising given the costly nature of the signaling as well as the structural similarity to the example in Section 2.5, where separation was sustained as equilibrium behavior. However Banks [17] shows that the pooling result does not generalize to an environment where the sender is uncertain about the preferences of receiver. Suppose we modify the above game by assuming R's ideal point x_i is a random variable drawn from $\mathbb{R}$ according to a twice continuously differentiable distribution $G(\cdot)$, with strictly positive density $g(\cdot)$. A strategy for R is now a function $r: M \times \mathbb{R} \rightarrow \Delta(A)$, where without loss of generality we assume that R adopts a pure strategy;[21] let $X_j(m) = \{x_i \in \mathbb{R}: r(a_j, m, x_i) = 1\}$, $j = 1, 2$. Then the expected utility for S from proposing $m \in M$, given type $t \in T$ and response r is

$$U_S(t, m, r) = \int_{X_1} u_s(m) \cdot g(x_i) dx_i + \int_{X_2} u_s(t) \cdot g(x_i) dx_i. \qquad (46)$$

The best response correspondence of R is

$$BR(\lambda, m, x_i) = \begin{cases} 1 & \text{if } x_i \geq x(\lambda, m) \\ 0 & \text{else} \end{cases}, \qquad (47)$$

where $x(\lambda, m)$ is defined in eq. (45). Now since x_i and t are drawn independently, in any sequential equilibrium the receiver's beliefs $\mu(m)$ will not be a function of x_i in or out of equilibrium, where this follows from an identical logic to that in Section 2.2 showing the equivalence of beliefs when there are multiple receivers. Therefore without loss of generality we can let the strategy for R be simply $r: \mathbb{R} \rightarrow \mathbb{R}$, where if $x_i < r(m)$ R rejects m and if $x_i > r(m)$ R accepts. The equilibrium condition for the receiver is then for all $m \in M$, $r(m) = x(\mu(m), m)$. With this notation the expected utility of the sender is then

$$U_S(t, m, r) = \int_{-\infty}^{r(m)} u_s(t) \cdot g(x_i) dx_i + \int_{r(m)}^{\infty} u_s(m) \cdot g(x_i) dx_i$$

$$= G(r(m)) \cdot u_s(t) + [1 - G(r(m))] \cdot u_s(m), \qquad (48)$$

which is utility equivalent to

---

[21] In equilibrium the set of indifferent types will have measure zero.

$$\tilde{U}_S(t, m, r) = [1 - G(r)] \cdot [u_s(m) - u_s(t)]. \tag{49}$$

Consider first the optimal behavior by S if t is known to R.[22] In this case, $x(\lambda, m) = (m + t)/2$, and

$$\tilde{U}_S(t, m, r) = [1 - G((m + t)/2)] \cdot [u_s(m) - u_s(t)]. \tag{50}$$

Thus with complete information concerning $t \in T$ the equilibrium proposal, $m^c(t)$, solves

$$\max_m \ [1 - G((m + t)/2)] \cdot [u_s(m) - u_s(t)]. \tag{51}$$

Suppose we make the common assumption that the hazard rate, $g(x)/[1 - G(x)]$, is non-decreasing in x; this plus the concavity of $u_s(\cdot)$ insures that the solution to (51) is unique. Banks [17] then employs the results of Mailath [49] to show that there exists a unique separating equilibrium to the incomplete information game; in addition this equilibrium is the only universally divine equilibrium. Therefore by sufficiently smoothing out the expected response by the receiver, we lose the pooling result found in Banks [13] and replace it with a separating result, implying a maximal amount of information transmitted through the proposal strategy of the sender. Further, since this equilibrium will not be a function of the prior belief $f(\cdot)$ (except for the determination of the support $[\underline{t}, \bar{t}]$), the negative relationship between the expected type and the equilibrium outcome in Banks [13] falls away as well.

Although it is not possible in general to solve for the separating strategy of S, it being the solution to a non-linear differential equation, the following characteristic holds: $m^*(\bar{t}) = m^c(\bar{t})$, and for all $t \in [\underline{t}, \bar{t})$ $m^*(t) < m^c(t)$. Thus there is a *downward* pressure on the equilibrium proposals relative to those offered with complete information, in contrast to the upward pressure in the Spence [78] model. In addition, this implies that the probability of acceptance is also higher than with complete information. Hence the ability of the agenda setter to implement higher outcomes is mitigated by the equilibrium constraints imposed on the separating strategy.

---

[22] This model is studied in Morton [58].

3.4. Legislative oversight of agencies

Banks [12] extends the Niskanen [63] model of budgetary agenda control to an environment where an agency possess an informational advantage *vis-à-vis* its oversight committee. A representative actor R plays the role of the committee, while the agency is S, the sender; S and R interact to determine the agency's budget. R has an inelastic demand for a single unit of S's services, where $v > 0$ is R's monetary value of the unit. The cost of the services is t, which is known *ex ante* to S but not to R; the prior is $f(\cdot)$ over $[0, v] = T$.[23]

As in Gilligan and Krehbiel [36] two procedures for determining the budget are analyzed: under the closed procedure the sender makes a budget request of $m \in \mathbb{R}$ to the receiver, who can then either, i) accept m, and thereby have the agency's budget set equal to m, ii) reject m, in which case no transaction occurs, or iii) audit the agency at a cost $k > 0$, which reveals t, and then set the budget equal to t. Under the open procedure R has in addition the ability to make a counteroffer to S, who then either accepts or rejects. Thus, in relation to the basic signalling model outlined in Section 2, a type is a cost of services, a message is a budget request by the agency, and the set of actions for the receiver consist of acceptance, rejection, auditing, and (in the open procedure) making a counterproposal. Both S and R are assumed to be risk-neutral, with S interested in maximizing the budget surplus $b - t$[24] and R maximizing his net benefits $v - b$ net of any auditing costs incurred; if no transaction occurs the payoffs to both players is set equal to zero.

Under the closed procedure the set of actions for R is $A = \{a_1, a_2, a_0\}$, where a_1 denotes accepting the proposed budget, a_2 denotes auditing, and a_0 rejection. Thus $r: \mathbb{R} \to \Delta(A)$ is the receiver's auditing strategy, where we let $r_i(m) = r(a_i; m)$, and $m: [0, v] \to \mathbb{R}$ is the sender's budget request strategy. The expected utilities of S and R are then $U_S(t, m, r) = r_1 \cdot (m - t)$, $U_S(\lambda, m, r) = r_1 \cdot (v - m) + r_2 \cdot (v - t_\lambda - k)$, and R's best response correspondence is

---

[23] We can ignore types greater than v since in no equilibria will they ever provide their services.

[24] By utility-equivalence, this is the same as S maximizing the expected budget.

$$BR(\lambda, m) = \begin{cases} (1, 0, 0) & \text{if } m < \min\{v, t_\lambda + k\} \\ (0, 1, 0) & \text{if } t_\lambda + k < \min\{v, m\} \\ (0, 0, 1) & \text{if } v > \max\{m, t_\lambda + k\}, \\ (x, 1 - x, 0) & \text{if } m = t_\lambda + k < v \\ (y, z, w) & \text{if } m = t_\lambda + k = v \end{cases} \qquad (52)$$

where $x, y, z, w \in [0, 1]$ and $y + z + w = 1$.

Thus without loss of generality we can restrict the budget proposals to $[0, v]$, since R will never accept any proposal greater than v.

Let k^* solve

$$\int_0^v t \cdot f(t) dt \bigg/ \int_0^v f(t) dt = v - k, \qquad (53)$$

so that if $k = k^*$ then R is indifferent between accepting and auditing a budget of v requested by all $t \in T$. Banks [12] then shows that if $k > k^*$ the unique universally divine equilibrium path is where $m^*(t) = v$ for all $t \in T$ and $r_1(m^*(t)) = 1$. Thus if the auditing costs of the legislator are sufficiently high the agency is able to extract all of the available rents in the form of an inflated budget. For all $k < k^*$ define t' as the cost which solves

$$\int_t^v t \cdot f(t) dt \bigg/ \int_t^v f(t) dt = v - k, \qquad (54)$$

so that if $m = v$ is requested by exactly those types in $[t', v]$, R will be indifferent between accepting and auditing. Then the following constitutes the unique universally divine equilibrium path: if $t \in [0, t']$ $m^*(t) = t + k$, $r_1^*(m^*(t)) = \exp\{-t/k\}$, and $r_2^*(m^*(t)) = 1 - r_1^*(m^*(t))$, so for relatively low types the sender's equilibrium strategy is separating and the receiver responds with a positive probability of both acceptance and auditing; if $t \in (t', v]$ $m^*(t) = v$, $r_1^*(t) = \exp\{-t'/k\} \cdot k/(v - t')$, and $r_2^*(t) = 1 - r_1^*(t)$, so relatively high types pool at $m = v$ and the receiver responds with positive probabilities of acceptance and auditing. From a distributional perspective, low types share the available rents with the receiver, since both players achieve strictly positive expected payoffs, while high types generate zero rents for the receiver.

Note the similarity in the strategies with those from the

Reinganum–Wilde [68] model in Section 2.5; in particular, the equilibrium auditing strategy is the solution to an analogous first-order differential equation. With a finite v, however, it is not possible for all cost types to separate since (according to $m(t) = t + k$) some types would have to request a budget greater than v, implying that R would surely reject. Therefore a subset of cost types pool at the highest possible acceptable request, namely $m = v$, where R must again be randomizing. This implies that the correct subset of types is (by monotonicity) the interval $[t', v]$.

There are two possible sources of (*ex post*) inefficiency in the interaction between S and R: no exchange, or R audits. The former is inefficient since with the cost t known to be less than the legislator's value v, there always exists a budget which both players find acceptable to no exchange; while the latter is inefficient since auditing leads to a budget which could have been implemented without auditing. From the above characterization of equilibrium behavior we see that if $k > k^*$ then the equilibrium is efficient, since an exchange always occurs and auditing never occurs, while if $k < k^*$ the equilibrium is inefficient, since even though an exchange again always takes place auditing occurs with positive probability for all $t \in (0, v]$. On the other hand, the equilibrium when $k > k^*$ generates a highly skewed distribution of payoffs, in that S receives the entire possible surplus from the exchange, whereas the distribution when $k < k^*$ is non-trivially divided among S and R. Indeed, as k approaches zero, S's payoff goes to zero and R's approaches the entire surplus. Thus there exists a fundamental trade-off between efficiency and equity in the interaction between S and R, where the extent of this trade-off is a function of the relative costliness of auditing.

Now consider the open procedure. A strategy for S will consist of a budget request $m: [0, v] \to \mathbb{R}$ and a response $\sigma: [0, v] \times \mathbb{R} \to [0, 1]$, where $\sigma(t, p)$ is the probability S accepts a counterproposal $p \in \mathbb{R}$ given cost t. Sequential rationality implies $\sigma(t, p) = 0$ if $p < t$ and $\sigma(t, p) = 1$ if $p > t$, so without loss of generality we can suppress this action choice. For R a strategy will give a decision to accept, reject, audit, or make a counterproposal following any budget request, as well as the amount of the counterproposal. We can without loss of generality simplify such a strategy by noting that rejecting a budget request is equivalent to making a counterproposal of $p = 0$, while accepting m is equivalent to a counterproposal of $p = m$. Therefore we can define a strategy for R as a pair of functions (r, ρ), where $r: \mathbb{R} \to [0, 1]$, $\rho: \mathbb{R} \to \mathbb{R}$, $r(m)$

describes the probability with which R makes a counterproposal, $\rho(m)$ gives the counterproposal, and $1 - r(m)$ is the probability of audit.

The sender's expected utility is then $U_S(t, m, r, p) = r \cdot (p - t)$ if $t \leq p$ and $U_S(t, m, r, p) = 0$ otherwise, since either R audits, in which case S sets the budget equal to t and S receives a payoff of zero, or R makes a counterproposal p, which S accepts if $t \leq p$ and rejects if $t > p$. Thus with the open procedure the signaling by S is costless. For the receiver, $U_R(\lambda, m, r, p) = r \cdot \int_0^p (v - p) \cdot \lambda(t) dt + (1 - r) \cdot (v - t_\lambda - k)$. The optimal counterproposal for R, given beliefs λ, is denoted $p(\lambda)$, where

$$p(\lambda) \in \underset{p}{\operatorname{argmax}} \int_0^p (v - p) \cdot \lambda(t) dt, \tag{55}$$

and we let $\pi(\lambda) \equiv \int_0^{p(\lambda)} (v - p(\lambda)) \cdot \lambda(t) dt$. Then R's optimal choice of r, which we denote as before $BR(\lambda, m)$, is

$$BR(\lambda, m) = \begin{cases} 1 & \text{if} & > \\ [0, 1] & \text{if } \pi(\lambda) = v - t_\lambda - k. \\ 0 & & < \end{cases} \tag{56}$$

As with the closed procedure the equilibrium behavior of the players will be a function of the relative costliness of auditing. Define k^{**} as the auditing cost which solves

$$\pi(f) = v - t_f - k. \tag{57}$$

If $k = k^{**}$, R is indifferent between auditing and making a counterproposal $p = p(f)$, given the prior belief $f(\cdot)$. Banks [12] shows that any equilibrium path is of the following form:[25] $m^*(t) = m \in [0, v]$ for all $t \in T$, and i) if $k > k^{**}$, $r^*(t) = 1$ and for $t \leq p(f)$ the budget is set equal to $p(f)$, while if $t > p(f)$ no exchange occurs; ii) if $k < k^{**}$, then $r^*(t) = 0$, so the legislator audits with probability 1. Therefore in any equilibrium the budget request strategy of the agency is completely uninformative. Thus, in addition to playing no substantive role in determining the agency's budget, the strategy plays no informational role as well. This contrasts with the result in Gilligan and Krehbiel [36], where the cause of the discrepancy is that in the current model the pre-

---

[25] To pin down the strategies Banks [12] assumes the auditing is slightly 'imperfect', defined below.

ferences of the players over budgets are diametrically opposed. Indeed, the pooling result follows the logic of Crawford and Sobel [28] outlined in Section 2.6 above: as the preferences of the players diverge in a costless signaling game it becomes less likely that any information gets transmitted. The current model then can be seen as an extreme case of preference divergence.

In terms of *ex post* efficiency we see that $k < k^{**}$ the outcome is always inefficient, since R always audits; yet an exchange always occurs as well. On the other hand, if $k \geq k^{**}$ R never audits, yet an exchange fails to take place when $t > p(f)$ even though an exchange at a price $p \in (t, v)$ would have been beneficial to both S and R. Thus the manifestation of the inefficiency inherent in the open process, namely auditing or failure to exchange, depends on the relative costliness of auditing to the committee.

In comparing the efficiency properties of the equilibria associated with the open and closed procedures, Banks [12] generates a result analogous to Gilligan and Krehbiel [36]. It is clear upon inspection of k^*, the critical value of the auditing cost for the closed procedure, is greater than k^{**}, the critical cost for the open procedure. Then we get the following result: If $k < k^{**}$, the *ex ante* expected utility of the legislator under the closed procedure is the same as that under the open procedure; further, if the auditing technology is 'imperfect', so that with some (small) probability the audit fails and the legislator must decide on either the proposed budget or no exchange, the former is strictly greater than the latter. Therefore the legislator has a preference for the closed procedure over the open even though the closed procedure limits the proposal-making ability of the legislator and hence assigns to the agency a greater degree of agenda control. In Gilligan and Krehbiel [36] this preference for a restrictive rule is due to the increased informativeness of the resulting equilibrium strategy by the sender, which is valuable given the receivers' risk aversion. In the current model however the receiver is risk-neutral, implying that such informational gains do not exist. On the other hand, the ability of the legislator to audit the agency's budget proposal and subsequently impose a budget equal to the true cost of services, serves to mitigate the ability of the agency to extract distributional gains emanating from its agenda control. In particular, under the closed rule the agency only attempts to extract the amount the legislator would forego by not auditing the agency, namely the auditing cost k. But since under the

open rule no information is transmitted that would persuade the
legislator not to audit, for $k < k**$ the legislator incurs the auditing cost
and thereby eliminates any distributional gains for the agency. From
this argument, it is also clear that for relatively low auditing costs the
agency strictly prefers the closed rule to the open regardless of the type
t, since under the former the agency receives a positive probability of
achieving a budget strictly greater than its cost.

4. RHETORIC AND DEBATE

4.1. Introduction

In the previous section we considered models that analyzed various
aspects of agenda control in a legislative environment. In particular,
the models of Gilligan and Krehbiel [36], [37]idemonstrated the impact
informational asymmetries can have on the decision making process
and output of a deliberative body such as Congress. Clearly, however,
there are avenues for information transmission and arenas for output
distortions due to incomplete information other than those studied by
Gilligan and Krehbiel. In what follows we consider some of these.

A common feature of many political interactions is the presence of
speeches, debates, etc. prior to a decision-making process. Typically
the assumption is that the content of these speeches does not in and of
itself effect the outcomes and utilities of the participants, but rather
that they provide a forum for transmitting and acquiring valuable
information for the subsequent utility-relevant decisions. Clearly,
complete information models are inadequate for the understanding of
the behavior owing to such possibilities, except perhaps in the role of
debate and cheap talk as a coordinating device among various equilibrium strategies (cf. Farrell [32]). A more appropriate model of such
phenomena would be one involving costless signaling, where as
discussed above the principle goal of such models is to measure the
ability of the participants to transmit valuable information in the
presence of the differing objectives.

The first model we examine, due to Matthews [50], is one in which a
representative actor from, e.g., Congress, is considering the selection
of a policy from $X \subset \mathbb{R}$. A second actor, e.g. the president, has veto
power over the former's choice, where a veto generates the status quo

outcome x. In addition, the President has the ability to make a speech prior to Congress' choice of policy, where we can think of this speech as selecting a message $m \in \mathbb{R}$ which, in effect, says, 'I will veto such and such policies.' With complete information concerning the President's preferences, Congress would ignore such a statement and simply choose its preferred policy among those preferred by the President to the status quo, as in the complete information models of agenda control discussed in Section 3.1. However if Congress is uncertain about the President's preferences, any information inferred from the speech will be incorporated into the optimal policy choice, and the relevant question then concerns the ability of the President to signal to the Congress her veto intentions, i.e. her preferences. Matthews [50] determines the extent of information transmission in such an environment according the equilibrium behavior of the participants in this costless signaling game.

Austen-Smith [4] considers an alternative model of speeches and debate within a legislature, wherein various individuals possess private information concerning the consequences of various legislative outcomes. As in the Gilligan and Krehbiel models, the assumption is that if the legislature selects an outcome $x \in X \subset \mathbb{R}$, the induced outcome or the consequence of selecting x is $x + t$, where t is a random variable. In the model of Austen-Smith [4] there are three legislators, all of whom possess some information concerning the realized value of the variable t. Each legislator has the ability to propose an outcome in X, and given the triple of proposals the legislators then vote to select an outcome. Hence the proposal stage provides a means of signaling private information, where this signaling is costly in that any proposal may ultimately be adopted. Prior to the proposal-making, however, each legislator has the opportunity to costlessly signal his information through a speech, thereby alleviating the potential dual role played by the proposals. Austen-Smith [4] then considers the relative informativeness of the speeches and the proposals, as well as the equilibrium outcomes in games with and without the debate stage.[26]

---

[26] See also Austen-Smith and Riker [8], [9]. In Austen-Smith [5] an equilibrium refinement related to the intuitive criterion is applied to the current model.

4.2. Veto Threats in Bargaining

In the Matthews [50] model the sender S and receiver R interact to determine an outcome from a unidimensional outcome space $X = \mathbb{R}$. The sequence of actions is as follows: S sends a message $m \in M$, after which R selects a proposal $\tilde{a} \in A = \mathbb{R}$; subsequently either S vetoes $\tilde{a}$, thereby generating the status quo outcome x_0, or S accepts $\tilde{a}$. We interpret a sender of type t as one who will accept the proposal $\tilde{a}$ if and only if $\tilde{a} \in [t, x_0]$ or $\tilde{a} \in [x_0, t]$ depending on whether $t \gtrless x_0$; let $T = [\underline{t}, \overline{t}] \subset \mathbb{R}$ denote the set of sender types and $f(\cdot)$ the receiver's prior belief over T. In general we describe the sender's preferences over X by a continuously differentiable function $u_s(\cdot, t)$, which is single-peaked at $z(t)$ for all t; further, assume $u_s(\cdot)$ satisfies the single-crossing property $\partial^2 u_s / \partial x \partial t > 0$. The receiver's preferences over outcomes are represented by a continuously differentiable and single-peaked utility function $u_r(\cdot)$ on X; let $x = 0$ be R's ideal outcome, so that $\partial u_r / \partial x \gtrless 0$ as $x \lessgtr 0$, and assume without loss of generality $x_0 > 0$.

Therefore we can model the situation as a signaling game where the preferences over $T \times M \times A$ are characterized by

$$U_i(t, m, a) = \begin{cases} u_i(a) & \text{if } a \in [t, x_0] \text{ or } a \in [x_0, t] \\ u_i(x_0) & \text{else} \end{cases}, \quad i = S, R.$$

(58)

If $t \in [\underline{t}, 0]$ then S is referred to as *accommodating*, in that S prefers R's ideal outcome $x = 0$ to the status quo; therefore if R knew S is accommodating R would simply propose $x = 0$ and S would not veto. If $t \in (0, x_0)$ S is *compromising*, since there exists outcomes (those in the interval (t, x_0)) which both S and R prefer to the status quo. However, if $t \in (0, x_0)$ were known to R, R's utility-maximizing proposal, $x = t$, would minimize S's utility, since S would be left indifferent between the status quo and the proposed outcome. Finally, if $t \in [x_0, \overline{t}]$, S is *recalcitrant*; no movement away from the status quo in the direction of R's ideal outcome is preferred by S. Since in equilibrium R's proposed outcome will be in $[0, x_0)$ and all recalcitrant types will veto, we can without loss of generality ignore such types and set $\overline{t} = x_0$, and $A = [0, x_0]$.

The game is one with costless signaling, so that for all $\lambda \in \Delta(T)$ and $m, m' \in M$, $BR(\lambda, m) = BR(\lambda, m')$. As noted above, if R proposes $\tilde{a}$ then types $t < \tilde{a}$ accept $\tilde{a}$ while types $t > \tilde{a}$ veto $\tilde{a}$. Therefore $BR(\lambda)$ maximizes

$$U_R(\lambda, m, a) = \int_{\underline{t}}^{a} u_R(a) \cdot \lambda(t) dt + \int_{a}^{\bar{t}} u_R(x_0) \cdot \lambda(t) dt$$

$$= \int_{\underline{t}}^{a} u_R(a) \cdot \lambda(t) dt + \left[1 - \int_{\underline{t}}^{a} \lambda(t) dt \right] \cdot u_R(x_0), \qquad (59)$$

which is utility equivalent to

$$\tilde{U}_R(\lambda, m, a) = \int_{\underline{t}}^{a} [u_R(a) - u_R(x_0)] \cdot \lambda(t) dt. \qquad (60)$$

Since the game is one with costless signaling, the fundamental issue is the informativeness of the sender's equilibrium strategy $m^*(\cdot)$. Naturally there exists uninformative 'babbling' equilibria, where the equilibrium proposal by R is simply $BR(f) \equiv a_f \in [0, x_0)$. Thus if $t \leq a_f$ S accepts, generating an outcome equal to a_f, while if $t > a_f$ S rejects, generating an outcome equal to x_0. The key is that in such equilibria the role of speechmaking is trivial; the equilibrium outcome is equivalent to that generated without speechmaking.

Matthews [50] then goes on to show that for some values of the parameters there also exist equilibria where some information gets transmitted. These equilibria are all equivalent to the following: $m^*(t) = m_1$ if $t \in [\underline{t}, \tau) \equiv T_1$, $m^*(t) = m_2$ if $t \in [\tau, \bar{t}] \equiv T_2$, where $m_1 \neq m_2$ and $\tau \in (\underline{t}, 0)$. Therefore if m_1 is observed the receiver infers the senders is an accommodating type, and proposes $a^*(m_1) = 0$; S subsequently accepts $a^*(m_1)$, since this is preferred to x_0 by all $t \in T_1$. On the other hand if m_2 is observed R places positive probability on S being either accommodating or compromising, and the optimal proposal $a^*(m_2)$ is strictly between 0 and x_0; hence with positive probability the 'compromise' proposal $a^*(m_2)$ is vetoed. Therefore in equilibrium the sender either reveals himself to be accommodating and the receiver's optimal outcome is implemented, or the sender informs the receiver that he is not 'extremely' accommodating, with the result being either the compromise proposal or the status quo.

Note that there does exist an equilibrium where S at times separates and reveals precisely his type t, where this equilibrium is 'outcome-equivalent' to that above and has the following path: if $t \in T_1$ then $m^*(t) = t$ and $a^*(t) = 0$, while if $t \in T_2$ $m^*(t) = t' > \tau$ and $a^*(t)$ equals the compromise proposal $a^*(m_2)$ above. Therefore if the sender is extremely accommodating she can reveal her type through the choice of message, where recall such separation was not a possibility in the costless signaling model of Crawford and Sobel [28] model discussed in Section 2.6. It is clear then that separation in the Matthews model hinges on the fact that the optimal response by the receiver is the same for all accommodating types, namely $a = 0$, where this 'flat' response was assumed away in the Crawford and Sobel model. Therefore, although separation is possible in the current model, such separation is not influential in that the additional information does not alter the receiver's optimal response; as long as the receiver knows the sender is accommodating, the precise value of S's type is irrelevant.

Alternatively, Matthews [50] shows that in any equilibrium all compromising types must pool together, thereby limiting the amount of information the receiver can potentially acquire. This conclusion follows from the fact that there can be at most one equilibrium proposal elicited in the interval $(0, x_0)$. Suppose on the contrary a_1 and a_2 are elicited in equilibrium, where $0 < a_1 < a_2 < x_0$. Then there exists a type $\tilde{t}$ such that $z(\tilde{t}) \in (a_1, a_2)$ and $u_s(a_1, \tilde{t}) = u_s(a_2, \tilde{t})$, implying $u_s(a_1, \tilde{t}) > u_s(x_0, \tilde{t})$, so $\tilde{t} < a_1$. Then since no type higher than $\tilde{t}$ elicits a_2, since higher types prefer higher outcomes, when R observes the message eliciting a_1, he places zero probability on types greater than $\tilde{t}$. Therefore by proposing $a' = a_1 - \epsilon$ R will generate the same probability of acceptance at a preferred (by R) outcome, leading to a contradiction. This then implies that if two proposals are elicited in equilibrium, both cannot be strictly above zero.

Therefore, in equilibrium, the receiver will never be able to distinguish compromising types, although R may be able to distinguish accommodating types. Suppose now that $t \geq 0$, so that R is certain that S is a compromiser. Then it follows that the only equilibria are completely uninformative, i.e. babbling. The logic of this result is identical to that above showing there cannot exist more than one compromise proposal elicited in equilibrium. In particular, the preferences of S and R are diametrically opposed on the set of jointly preferable outcomes $(t, x_0]$; revealing any information about this set will not be consistent with equilibrium behavior. This pooling result is similar to the result in Crawford and Sobel [28] where the degree of divergence in the players' preferences dictated the degree of informativeness of the sender's strategy.

Thus the ability of Congress to infer *any* information through the speech by the President is predicated on the existence of accommodating Presidential types, that is, types which prefer Congress's ideal outcome to the status quo. Further, the extent of such information is limited to selecting out the most extreme accommodating types, without providing any information about compromising types. On the other hand, this information is sufficient to generate an additional, and somewhat paradoxical, equilibrium prediction: whenever Congress proposes its utility-maximizing outcome the President never vetoes, whereas when Congress proposes a compromise outcome the President vetoes with positive probability. The rationale behind this is that Congress only proposes its utility maximizing outcome when it is assured the President will accept; otherwise Congress infers the presence of compromising types and hedges by proposing an outcome strictly greater than zero. Yet the optimal compromise proposal is sensitive to the tradeoff between proposing an outcome with a higher probability of acceptance versus proposing an outcome which is preferable conditional on being accepted. In equilibrium Congress never arrives at a 'corner' solution to this problem, and hence finds its compromise proposal vetoed by some types of President.

In this manner, we see the effect of allowing the President the opportunity to signal his veto intentions through speech-making. Although precise and influential information can never be transmitted through the speeches, for some parameter values the President is able to influence the equilibrium outcome by transmitting valuable information to Congress.

4.3. Debate, proposals, and voting

The game analyzed in Austen-Smith [4] differs from the typical sender/receiver games previously considered, in that potentially all players both send and receive private information. The structure of the game is as follows: there are three players, $N = \{1, 2, 3\}$, who jointly decide on an outcome from a unidimensional outcome space $X = \mathbb{R}$. Player i's preferences over X are characterized by the function $u_i(x) = -(x_i - x)^2$, $i = 1, 2, 3$; let $x_1 < x_2 = 0 < x_3$ denote the players' ideal outcomes. Incomplete information exists to the extent that if the players jointly select a bill $b \in \mathbb{R}$, the resulting outcome is $x(b, t) = b + \tilde{\tau}$, where $\tilde{\tau}$ is the realized value of a random variable τ, and where τ is distributed according to a Bernoulli distribution with parameter q. Thus the realized value of τ is either 0 or 1, and $E(\tau) = q$. The parameter q is unknown, with the players having a common prior on q given by a Beta distribution with parameters $\alpha = \beta = 1$, implying the prior belief that $q = 1/2$. Asymmetric information exists in that each $i \in N$ observes an independent draw t_i from the distribution of τ, so that $t_i \in \{0, 1\} \equiv T_i$ is player i's type; let $t = (t_1, t_2, t_3)$ be the realized or true type profile of the players. Note that even if t were known to all players there would still exist a 'residual' uncertainty concerning the value of τ; however such uncertainty would be symmetrically held by the players and hence would be irrelevant from a behavioral standpoint. So we will refer to the case where t is common knowledge as the 'complete information' case.

Upon observing t_i, player i's induced preferences over the set of bills $B = \mathbb{R}$ is given by $- (x_i - 1/3 \cdot (1 + t_i) - b)^2 - \text{var}(\tau; t_i)$; i.e. if $t_i = 0$, i's induced ideal point is $x_i - 1/3$, while if $t_i = 1$ it is $x_i - 2/3$. In addition, if $t_i = 0$ player i places greater probability that $t_j = 0$ than $t_j = 1$, $j \neq i$, and similarly if $t_i = 1$. Thus the players' types, and hence their induced preferences over B, are positively correlated, providing an incentive to 'share' information. However, as we shall see, their divergence of preferences will provide an opposite incentive to 'withhold' information, and the relevant question concerning the informativeness of the players' strategies then hinges on which of these incentive effects outweighs the other.

The decision-making process has three stages:

The *debate stage*, in which i selects a message m_i from a set M;
The *proposal stage*, where i selects a proposed bill $b_i \in B$;
the *voting stage*, where i reports a single-peaked ranking of $b = (b_1, b_2, b_3)$.

The resulting social decision then is the Condorcet winner among $\{b_1, b_2, b_3\}$, i.e. the bill that constitutes a majority winner against the other alternatives, when considered in pairwise comparisons according to the rankings selected. If no such bill exists a fair lottery over the weak Condorcet set determines the final bill.

At each stage players act simultaneously, and only pure strategies are considered. A strategy for i is thus a triple (m_i, b_i, v_i), where

$$m_i: T_i \to M,$$
$$b_i: T_i \times M^3 \to B,$$

$$v_i: T_i \times M^3 \times B^3 \rightarrow \{\text{single-peaked orderings of } B\}.$$

Thus $m_i(t_i)$ is the message sent by i of type t_i; $b_i(t_i, m)$ is the proposed bill by i given type t_i and messages $m = (m_1, m_2, m_3)$, and $v_i(t_i, m, b)$ is the voting rule employed given type t_i, messages m, and bills b.

Austen-Smith [4] considers two different message sets, $M(1)$ and $M(2)$, where $|M(j)| = j$. Thus if $M = M(1)$ the debate stage is vacuous, in that there is only one possible message; refer to this game as the game *without* debate. If $M = M(2)$ there exists the possibility that a player may signal her type through her choice of message; refer to this as the game *with* debate. Since only pure strategies are considered the assumption that the debate game consists of only two possible messages is without loss of generality.

Note that in *either* game there exists the possibility of player i signaling t_i through the proposed bill b_i, where such signaling would be 'costly' as defined in Section 2. In the game with debate player i has in addition the possibility of costlessly signaling t_i, since the messages do not directly effect the outcome of the decision process. In either game therefore there exists separating strategies which reveal to the remaining players t_i, where such information is useful at the voting stage as well as the proposal stage (if revealed in debate).

The definition of sequential equilibrium in this game is obviously more complex than that derived in Section 2.2 for signaling games, and hence we refrain from going into the details. However the general principles of sequential rationality and consistency remain: at each stage, players select their actions optimally given their types, their beliefs about others' types, and the subsequent strategy choices. Further, along the equilibrium path the beliefs are required to satisfy Bayes' Rule.[27]

Austen-Smith [4] considers three classes of questions: 1) in either game, does information get revealed by the equilibrium strategies of the players? 2) if information is revealed in the debate game, is it at the proposal stage or the debate stage? 3) what is the relationship between the equilibrium outcomes in the two games, as well as to the game with 'symmetric' information? In particular, the last question is concerned with the following: let $b(t) = E(\tau; t)$ be the induced ideal point of $i = 2$

---

[27] An additional assumption, common to most voting games, is that players never use weakly dominated strategies, since otherwise with majority rule there always exist equilibria where everybody votes for the same alternative regardless of preferences.

if all information is aggregated. Then with complete information (i.e. t = (t_1, t_2, t_3) common knowledge) it is easily seen that the resulting (unique) equilibrium final bill of the game would be $b(t)$, since this is the preferred bill of the median voter. Question three above can then be rephrased as, how often is the equilibrium final bill in the game with incomplete information (i.e. t_i private information) equal to $b(t)$?

The answers to the above questions rely not surprisingly on the degree to which the players' preferences coincide. Say that the preferences are *homogeneous* if $|x_i| \le 1/15$, $i = 1, 3$, while they are *heterogeneous* if $|x_i| > 2/3$. Austen-Smith [4] shows that regardless of whether the preferences are heterogeneous or homogeneous the (*ex ante*) median voter, player 2, always has a (weak) incentive to reveal his private information as soon as possible. Thus in any equilibrium with or without debate $b_2^*(0) \ne b_2^*(1)$, and with debate if $m_2^*(0) = m_2^*(1)$ is part of an equilibrium profile then a profile which differs from the original only in that $m_2^*(0) \ne m_2^*(1)$ is an equilibrium as well. This incentive to separate follows by the positive correlation of the players' types and the advantaged position of the median voter in terms of outcomes from the voting stage. Hereafter, then, we focus on the informativeness of the extreme voters, players 1 and 3.

Austen-Smith [4] proves the following: if preferences are heterogeneous then in any equilibrium of the game without debate, $b_i^*(0) = b_i^*(1)$, $i = 1, 3$, so that the median voter separates but the extreme voters pool, and the probability the equilibrium final bill is equal to $b(t)$ is zero. In any equilibrium in the game with debate, $m_i^*(0) = m_i^*(1)$ and $b_i^*(0) = b_i^*(1)$, $i = 1, 3$ so the only player that ever separates is the median voter. In addition, the final bill with debate coincides precisely with that generated without debate, and hence never equals $b(t)$. Therefore with heterogeneous preferences debate plays no informational role in the determination of the final outcome; further, with or without debate the players' proposals play no informational role. Therefore with heterogeneous preferences the 'pooling' incentives implied by the players' diverse preferences outweights the 'separating' incentives implied by the correlation of types. Note that this pooling result when preferences are diverse is similar in spirit to that in Crawford and Sobel [28], where in the current model this result is extended to include the costly signaling at the proposal stage as well.

Suppose on the other hand the players' preferences are homogeneous; then there exists an equilibrium in the game without debate where $b_i^*(0) \neq b_i^*(1)$ $i = 1$, 3, so that all players separate, and the probability the final bill equals $b(t)$ is $1/2$. In particular, in four of the eight possible realizations of the vector $t = (t_1, t_2, t_3)$ the information revealed and the bills proposed are such that the median voter's complete information induced ideal point is offered at the proposal stage, and is subsequently selected at the voting stage. Further, there exists an equilibrium in the game with debate such that $m_i^*(0) \neq m_i^*(1)$ $i = 1$, 3, so that all players reveal their type at the debate stage; the probability the final bill equals $b(t)$ is then equal to 1. The reason for the latter result is that the information concerning the vector t is revealed early enough in the process so that the equilibrium proposals can be conditioned on this information; in particular the median voter can propose her complete information induced ideal point, which is subsequently accepted at the voting stage. Without the debate stage the information concerning t_1 and t_3 is revealed 'in time' to select the median voter's preferred outcome under symmetric information *given the set of equilibrium proposals*, but 'too late' for the equilibrium proposal by, in particular, the median voter to incorporate this information. Therefore the final bill coincides with $b(t)$ only when player 2's conjectures about these values lead to the correct decision *ex post*.

Summarizing these results, we see that when preferences are homogeneous the advantage of the debate stage is that the relevant information concerning induced preferences is revealed earlier than without debate, where in the latter game the informativeness of the strategy is mixed in with the issue of offering an optimal proposal given knowledge only of t_i. On the other hand the presence of a debate stage with heterogeneous preferences does not imply a resulting (social) gain; if the players did not have the incentive to reveal the information through their proposals in the game without debate, then they do not have the incentive to reveal the information at the debate stage either. Thus the main conclusion from Austen-Smith [4] is as follows: 'debate does not elicit information that otherwise would not be made available during the decision-making process. Instead, it allows individuals to share their private data in time for it to be used at the agenda setting stage rather than only at the voting stage. It is precisely this timing role that yields an improvement (from a social decision-making perspective) over the game with no debate.'

5. ELECTORAL COMPETITION

5.1. Introduction

One of the principal substantive concerns of political scientists is the selection by voters of an agent to represent their interests in a legislature, and the subsequent competition by agents for the role of representative. The standard complete information model of two-candidate electoral competition due to Hotelling [43] and Downs [31] is as follows: there exists a set $N = \{1, \ldots, n\}$ of voters, n odd, a set $C = \{A, B\}$ of candidates, and a space $X \subset \mathbb{R}$ of outcomes. Voters have preferences defined over outcomes: $u_i: X \to \mathbb{R}$, while in general candidates have preferences defined over outcomes as well as who wins the election: $u_j: X \times C \to \mathbb{R}$. A strategy for candidate j is an element $m_j \in X$, while for a voter a strategy is $r_i: X \times X \to [0, 1]$, where $r_i(m_a, m_b)$ is the probability i votes for candidate A given announcements (m_a, m_b). Finally, an outcome $x \in X$ is determined, where the standard assumption is that x is simply equal to the announcement m_j of the candidate receiving a majority of the votes.

The following assumptions are also common: i) voter i's utility over outcome x is a decreasing function of the distance between x and i's 'ideal' outcome y_i, and ii) voters play weakly dominant 'anonymous' strategies, so that in equilibrium

$$r_i(m_a, m_b) = \begin{Bmatrix} 1 \\ 1/2 \\ 0 \end{Bmatrix} \text{ as } d(m_a, y_i) \begin{Bmatrix} < \\ = \\ > \end{Bmatrix} d(m_b, y_i).$$

Thus the vector $y = (y_1, \ldots, y_n)$ is sufficient to determine the behavior of the voters for any announcement pair (m_a, m_b).

With a one-dimensional outcome space and complete information the median voter theorem states that the equilibrium of the game will have both candidates adopting the median voter's ideal outcome, with each candidate winning the election with probability one-half. Extensions of this model incorporating incomplete information have generally fallen into one of two categories, depending on the characteristics of the informational asymmetries involved. Some previous models examine voter uncertainty concerning the preferences and behavior of the candidates, where the candidates' strategic role has been suppressed; see Calvert [23] for a survey. In these models the basic issue concerns the voters learning about the behavior of the candidates through repeated sampling. In the models of Harrington [40] and Banks [14] described below, such learning is present in augmented versions of the standard model outlined above by assuming that, i) each candidate is aware of the outcome x to be implemented if elected, and ii) the other candidate as well as the voters are unaware of this outcome *ex ante*. The voters thus face an 'adverse selection' problem in determining the preferred candidate, and the central issue concerns the willingness and ability of the candidates to mitigate this problem by signaling their intentions through their electoral announcements.

In addition, there have been numerous electoral models which add to the standard environment uncertainty concerning the *voters'* preferences, as characterized by the voter y; again see Calvert [23]. Assuming such uncertainty is shared symmetrically amongst the candidates their strategies play no informational role, and given the sequence of actions outlined above there is clearly no avenue for the voters to 'signal' their preferences to the candidates. In the model of Ledyard [48] described below, this environment is augmented by assuming that, i) each candidate possesses some information related to the vector y, ii) this information potentially differs across candidates, and iii) the candidates simultaneously make announcements at times $t = 1, 2$ prior to the election, where the winning candidate's announcement at time $t = 2$ is equal to the outcome x, and the announcements at $t = 1$ are 'costless'. Thus at $t = 1$ the candidates are potentially signaling their information to one another, where the voters ignore these announcements in determining their optimal voting strategy. The relevant issue then is whether the basic electoral mechanism provides the incentives for the candidates to transmit information to one another given the conflict between their collective preference for greater information and their diametrically opposed interests in the electoral outcomes.

5.2. Voter uncertainty

The sequence of events in the model of Harrington [40] is as follows: candidate j observes his type $t_j \in T_j$, and then makes an electoral announcement $m_j \in X \subset \mathbb{R}$. The candidates choose their announcements simultaneously, so the only signaling is between the candidates and the voters, and we restrict attention to pure strategies by the candidates. We can think of a candidate type as specifying the preferences over X of the candidate, e.g. t_j is candidate j's ideal outcome in X. The set of candidate types $T = T_a = T_b$ is assumed to be finite, as is X, and candidate types are drawn independently according to the probability $f(\cdot)$. As in the standard model voter i observes (m_a, m_b) and then votes for either A or B. If candidate j is elected, then the outcome is x with probability $h(x, t_j)$, so the signaling by the candidates is costless. In particular, the message pair (m_a, m_b) does not enter into the voters' utility functions; hence given beliefs $\mu_a(m_a)$, $\mu_b(m_b)$ about the candidates' types the voters' best response is determined by the expected utility associated with the functions $h(\cdot)$ and $\mu_j(\cdot)$. Candidate preferences are in general defined over the winning candidate, the outcome, and the candidate's type: $u_j: T_j \times X \times C \to \mathbb{R}$, while voter preferences are single-peaked on X.

As noted in Section 2.6 costless signaling games always possess pooling equilibria, and the model of Harrington [40] is no exception. The insight in the current model is that such pooling persists even in the presence of competition by another 'sender' who is also attempting to influence the voters' decisions. Suppose we now make the assumption that the candidates are solely office-motivated, implying $u_j(t_j, x, j) = \hat{u}_j(j) > \hat{u}_j(k) = u_j(t_j, x, k)$ for all $(t_j, x) \in T_j \times X, j \in \{A, B\}$. Then Harrington [40] shows that (generically) there exist no equilibria other than pooling equilibria. Thus if the candidates only care about winning the election, no information is ever revealed in their electoral announcements. This follows since if the voters' response strategies discriminate among the candidates as a function of the messages sent, as would happen 'generically' with non-pooling strategies, then given their office-motivated preferences all candidate types would have an incentive to send the message with the greatest associated probability of election. But this contradicts the assumption of information transmission in equilibrium.

Suppose on the other hand that we do not restrict candidate preferences, but rather assume the winning candidate implements her desired outcome with probability one, $h(t_j, t_j) = 1$. In addition, suppose we restrict attention to candidate strategies which are *identical*, i.e. $m_a^*(t) = m_b^*(t)$ for all $t \in T$, and *connected*, i.e. if $m_j^*(t) = m_j^*(t')$, then $\forall \tau \in (t, t') \, m_j^*(\tau) = m_j^*(t)$. Then Harrington [40] shows that the same result holds: only pooling equilibria exist. Hence, even when the candidates care about policy outcomes as well as getting elected, the electoral mechanism still does not provide the incentive for information revelation by the candidates. In particular, the adverse selection problem faced by the voters is the same regardless of whether electoral announcements are used as signaling devices by the candidates.[28]

The assumption so far has been that the sets T and X are finite. Harrington [40] notes that if instead X and T are intervals on the real line then the pooling result no longer holds. To see this, suppose that $X = T = [0, 1]$, $f(\cdot)$ is uniform, candidates are solely office-motivated, and the median voter's ideal point is equal to $1/2$. Then the following candidate strategies constitute an equilibrium:

$$m_j^*(t) = \begin{cases} m & \text{if } t \leq 1/2 \\ m' \neq m & \text{else} \end{cases}, j = a, b. \qquad (61)$$

Then if (m, m) or (m', m') is observed the median voter is indifferent between selecting either candidate, and hence each candidate is elected with probability $1/2$; a similar result holds if (m, m') or (m', m) is observed. Therefore candidate j of type t_j is indifferent between announcing m and m' for all $t_j \in T$, implying the above strategy is optimal given that the other candidate plays it as well. Further, the strategy reveals information to the voters: if candidate j sends m, then the voters are certain j's type is in the interval $[0, 1/2]$, while if j sends m' the voters infer j's type is in $[1/2, 1]$.

The key to the strategies above constituting equilibrium behavior on the part of the candidates, and the key to the difference between this non-pooling result with continuous T and X versus pooling with finite T and X, is that the information revealed by the strategy $m_a^*(\cdot)$ in conjunction with that revealed by $m_b^*(\cdot)$ implies the median voter is indifferent between the candidates for any pair of equilibrium messages. Therefore the information revealed by the candidates is 'useless' from the voters' perspective since it never assists in discriminating the candidates with regard to which will implement the preferred outcome. Thus the adverse selection problem persists after the messages are sent. With

---

[28] Harrington [40] goes on to consider additional restrictions on preferences and the function $h(\cdot)$ in order to get information revelation in equilibrium, and in fact shows that with certain restrictions separating equilibria exist.

finite sets this indifference can generically never occur, since a partition of T does not in general exist wherein the median voter is indifferent between electing a candidate whose type is known to be in one element of the partition and the opponent known to be in another element. Thus, although information does get transmitted with continuous types, from the voter's perspectives as well as the candidates' the strategies are *essentially* pooling strategies since the information revealed is useless to the voters and the probability of election is the same for all equilibrium messages. On the other hand, this also provides an explanation for how information can be observed to be transmitted in an environment where the incentives of the senders would seem to imply that *no* information could be revealed: any such information is useless.

Banks [14] takes a different approach to candidate signaling by incorporating a cost to the winning candidate from making an electoral announcement different from what is ultimately adopted. Candidate types are again drawn independently from T, where now T and X coincide and are a closed interval on $\mathbb{R}$ centered at the origin: $T = X = [-D, D]$. The prior $f(\cdot)$ is assumed symmetric about zero, which is also the location of the median voter's ideal point. The outcome associated with candidate j of type t_j winning the election is simply t_j. The principle difference with the model of Harrington [40] is in the specification of the candidates' utilities, which are now explicitly a function of the (winning) candidate's announcement. Thus $u_j : T \times M \times C \to \mathbb{R}$, where

$$u_j(t_j, m_j, k) = \begin{cases} \varphi(t_j, m_j) & \text{if } k = j \\ 0 & \text{else} \end{cases},$$

and $\varphi(\cdot)$ is assumed to be a strictly decreasing function of the distance between t_j and m_j. The rationale is that candidates do not possess policy preferences *per se*; yet their utility subsequent to winning the current election, for example in future elections, is a function of the degree to which the announced outcome differs from that actually implemented. Further, a losing candidate's payoff is not a function of either the outcome chosen by the winning candidate, or the losing candidates' type, since the latter is never verified and hence plays no role in, e.g., subsequent elections. The function $\varphi(\cdot)$ is parameterized by k, where $\partial \varphi(t, t)/\partial k = 0$, $\partial \varphi(t, m)/\partial k < 0 \ \forall t \neq m$, and $\partial^2 \varphi(t, m)/\partial k \partial m \lesseqgtr 0$ as $m \lesseqgtr t$. Thus k measures the degree of concavity of $\varphi(\cdot)$, so that as k increases $\varphi(\cdot)$ becomes narrower, implying a strictly higher cost from adopting an announcement $m \neq t_j$. As long as $k > 0$ any signaling by the candidates is costly. On the other hand, as in Harrington [40], the messages (m_a, m_b) do not effect the *voters'* utility, so their best response functions will be the same for all possible message pairs up to the posterior beliefs about candidate types. Banks [14] assumes voters have quadratic utilities over $\mathbb{R}$; hence, as in Section 3.2, the median voter is decisive in any sequential equilibrium, so that given beliefs $\mu_a(m_a)$, $\mu_b(m_b)$ candidate A wins if $-t_{\mu_a}^2 - \sigma_{\mu_a}^2 < -t_{\mu_b}^2 - \sigma_{\mu_b}^2$, and similarly for candidate B.

Banks [14] restricts attention to equilibria which are, i) *identical* across candidates, $m_a^*(t_a) = m_b^*(t_b) = m^*(t)$, ii) *symmetric* about the origin, $m^*(t) = -m^*(-t)$. Let k^* denote the value of k such that $\varphi(D, 0; k) = 0$, i.e. if $k = k^*$ then the most extreme type of candidate is indifferent between announcing the median position and subsequently winning the election, and simply losing the election. Then Banks [14] shows that the following constitute the unique universally divine equilibrium strategies for the candidates: if $k \leq k^*$, then $m^*(t) = 0 \; \forall \; t \in T$, while if $k > k^*$, then there exists $t(k) \in (0, D)$ such that $m^*(t) = 0 \; \forall \; t \in [-t(k), t(k)]$, and $m^*(t)$ is strictly increasing, i.e. separating, otherwise.[29] Thus for relatively low costs the candidates' strategies are uninformative, implying the voters remain indifferent between the two candidates. Note that as k approaches zero the specification of the model approaches that in Harrington [40] with office-motivated candidates, so we can think of Harrington's pooling result as being robust to small costs imposed on the signaling. On the other hand, with relatively high costs, 'extreme' candidates (i.e. $t < -t(k)$ or $t > t(k)$) will separate and reveal to the voters the outcome to be implemented, while 'moderate' types (i.e. $t \in [-t(k), t(k)]$) pool. Therefore if both candidates are extreme or one is extreme and the other is moderate the voters will select the 'correct' candidate. Hence the adverse selection problem exists only when both candidates are moderate. Further, the critical value $t(k)$ is decreasing in k, so that as the cost of announcing a policy different from t increases more types separate, thereby increasing the probability of the voters selecting the correct candidate. As k

---

[29] As in the Spence [78] model described in Section 2.5, the first-order differential equation describing the separating equilibrium is in this case non-linear and hence not explicitly solvable in general.

approaches infinity $t(k)$ approaches zero, implying all types separate. Therefore as the costliness of announcing a policy different from the true policy increases the electoral mechanism provides a greater incentive for the candidates to reveal this policy through their electoral announcements. At the other extreme is the model of Harrington [40] wherein with costless signaling the candidates never have the incentive to reveal this information. This comparison suggests that the informativeness of candidate strategies in elections, and the associated degree to which the voters' adverse selection problem is mitigated, will be measured by the extent penalties for 'deceptive' announcements influence the candidates' current expected payoffs. The voters certainly have the willingness to provide such penalties, since it is easily seen that, in particular, the median voter's *ex ante* expected payoff is increasing in k. What remains unanswered then is the ability of the voters to provide these incentives 'credibly' through, e.g., subsequent voting behavior.[30]

5.3. Candidate uncertainty

The model of electoral competition in Ledyard [48] differs from those of Harrington [40] and Banks [14] in that the focus is on *candidate* uncertainty about *voter* preferences. Ledyard also assumes each candidate possesses private information concerning these preferences and has the ability to signal to his opponent this information. Candidate j observes his type $t_j \in T_j$, where the triple (t_a, t_b, y) is drawn from $T_a \times T_b \times X$ according to some distribution $F(\cdot)$. At times $\tau = 1$, 2 candidates simultaneously make announcements from the set $X \subset \mathbb{R}$, where at $\tau = 2$ the $\tau = 1$ announcements are common knowledge. Thus a (pure) strategy for candidate j is a pair (m_j^1, m_j^2), where

$$m_j^1: T_j \to X,$$
$$m_j^2: T_j \times X \to X.$$

Thus $m_j^1(t_j)$ is the announcement of candidate j at $\tau = 1$ with type t_j, and $m_j^2(t_j, m_k)$ is the $\tau = 2$ announcement conditional on observing candidate k's $\tau = 1$ announcement of m_k, $k \neq j$. Rather than modelling the voters' decisions explicitly, Ledyard [48] summarizes their

---

[30] Ferejohn [34] and Austen-Smith and Banks [7] study this question in the context of a moral hazard, rather than adverse selection, problem.

decisions in a reduced form expression $\Pi(m_a, m_b, y)$, where this gives the probability of candidate A winning the election given $\tau = 2$ announcements (m_a, m_b) and voter preferences y. Further, we assume candidates are solely office-motivated, so without loss of generality we can let $\Pi(\cdot)$ and $-\Pi(\cdot)$ denote the payoffs to candidates' A and B, respectively, where $\Pi(\cdot)$ is assumed to have the usual symmetry and anonymity properties. Thus we can safely ignore the voters and focus attention on the game played by the candidates at $\tau = 1, 2$, where both are potential 'senders' and 'receivers' of information.

Note that if t_a and t_b are drawn independently of y neither candidate has any useful information to signal to the other; a similar conclusion holds if t_a and t_b are perfectly correlated, since even if they are in addition correlated with y the candidates' information prior to playing the game is identical. Now suppose t_a, t_b, and y are not drawn independent of one another, so the value of t_k is useful information for candidate j (e.g. j becomes better informed about the location of the median voter). Upon observing t_j candidate j non-trivially updates his belief concerning candidate k's type as well as the voters' preferences. Further, these beliefs may themselves be updated at $\tau = 2$ upon observing the announcement by candidate k at $\tau = 1$. Therefore if in equilibrium candidate k's $\tau = 1$ strategy is non-pooling, candidate j's posterior beliefs about, in particular, the parameter y may differ according to the observed $\tau = 1$ announcement of k, implying a different and 'more informed' (relative to the $\tau = 1$ beliefs) $\tau = 2$ announcement by j.

The key issue then concerns the informativeness of the $\tau = 1$ strategies by the candidates. Since the game involves costless signaling the usual result holds, namely, there exist pooling equilibria in which no information is revealed. Ledyard [48] then goes on to show that, although it is possible to have non-pooling equilibrium strategies, as in the model of Harrington [40] with continuous types any such strategies must be essentially pooling strategies. In particular, in any non-pooling equilibrium the probability of election is the same for all types and all equilibrium announcements given the candidates' updated information at $\tau = 1$. Therefore any information revealed by candidate j cannot be used by candidate k to select $\tau = 2$ announcements which bias the electoral outcome in k's favor, since otherwise no type would send the 'unfavorable' announcements.

As in earlier sections Ledyard's result can be seen as an extension of

the Crawford and Sobel [28] theorem which states that if the preferences of the sender and receiver are diametrically opposed no
information is transmitted. In the current model the preferences of the
candidates are diametrically opposed; hence, while some information
can be revealed in equilbrium, it cannot by its nature be 'useful' to the
receiver of the information.[31] However, as with the Harrington [40]
model, the existence of non-pooling equilibrium strategies also
provides an explanation for why information can be seen to be revealed
by the electoral announcements of the candidates: the explanation is
that such information is *strategically useless*.

From the above description, then, the results of Ledyard [48] fit well
with those of Harrington [40]: when signaling is costless, useful
information concerning a candidates' private knowledge about voter
preferences or his intentions once in office is not revealed through the
electoral mechanism. Banks [14] shows that the conclusions of
Harrington [40] differ if the signaling about candidate intentions is
made sufficiently costly. Hence a reasonable conjecture would be that
if, for example, the voters' decision rule over the selection of
candidates in the Ledyard [48] model was a function of both $\tau = 1$ and
$\tau = 2$ announcements, useful information may be revealed in equilibrium. Alternatively, Ledyard [48] explores a model with a sequence of
elections where in each election candidates make a single announcement, and where as above this is used by the voters to determine a
winner. Assuming candidates care about the outcomes in all elections,
the incentive for candidate j not to reveal t_j in any election, since this
information could then be used against j in subsequent elections, is
potentially offset by the incentive to use the information in the current
election to select a probability-maximizing choice of announcement.
Hence, as Ledyard [48] shows by way of example, there may exist
useful information transmission across elections, where although the
preferences of the candidates remain diametrically opposed the
signaling by the candidates is now costly.

Thus, as in the earlier models, we see how the electoral mechanism
'works' in achieving the revelation and aggregation of useful information only when the informed candidates incur some differential

---

[31] This feature differs somewhat from Harrington [40], where the preferences of the
receivers, i.e. the voters, are not necessarily opposed to any one candidate.

electoral costs to sending different messages. Without these costs the incentives derived solely from the competition among the candidates for the role as representative are insufficient for, and indeed are contrary to, the transmission of useful information by the candidates.

6. REPUTATION AND LEADERSHIP

6.1. Introduction

A common problem studied in both economics and political science is the ability of agents to influence the behavior of others through credibly threatening to punish the latter in the future for actions that are unacceptable to the agent. A well-known application of this in economics is the chain-store paradox (Selten [76]): a monopolist faces the prospect of entry in its markets by a finite set of potential entrants (one per market) at fixed time intervals. The monopolist prefers that no firms enter, and has at its disposal the ability to engage any entrant in a profit-draining price war upon entry. Although such a price war generates lower profits for the monopolist at the time, the common wisdom was that it would be beneficial to the monopolist to respond to entry in the earlier periods with such price wars to gain a reputation for fighting in the eyes of future entrants and thereby forestall any further entry (cf. Scherer [75]).

The 'paradox' of the story is of course a function of the finite time horizon and the presence of complete information (as well as the requirement that the equilibrium be subgame perfect): in the 'last' market the monopolist will have no incentive to engage in a price war, since there are no future entrants to influence; therefore the last entrant will surely enter, implying that in the penultimate market the mono-polist cannot influence the behavior of the last entrant, and so prefers not to engage in a price war and the penultimate entrant enters, etc. Using this backward induction we see how the game unravels, with the unique equilibrium behavior being that all potential entrants enter and the monopolist never engages in price wars.

Thus, as with the limit pricing example in Section 1, the predictions from the equilibrium analysis in a complete information environment ran counter to the common wisdom on the subject. And, again as with limit pricing, one 'solution' to this problem was found by assuming the

presence of incomplete information: Kreps and Wilson [47] and
Milgrom and Roberts [54] show that if with positive probability the
monopolist actually prefers to engage in a price war in any one market,
then this uncertainty about the monopolist's preferences can be
sufficient to generate price wars and reputation building as equilibrium
phenomena.

In Calvert [24] and Alt, Calvert, and Humes [2] a model is analyzed
which is a variation of the model in Kreps and Wilson [47]. The
scenario in Calvert [24] is one in which a political leader is attempting
to influence the behavior of a set of followers, whereas in Alt, Calvert,
and Humes [2] a relatively large nation or 'hegemon' seeks stability in
its regime by keeping the other members in line. Both papers however
employ the same basic structure, and so we will examine them jointly in
the next section.

6.2. The model

The model of Calvert [24] and Alt, Calvert, and Humes [2] consists of
two time periods in which agents select actions. There are three players,
1, 2, and S, where at time $i = 1$, 2, player i selects an action $a_i \in A = \{a_0, a_r\}$, where a_0 denotes 'obey' and a_r 'rebel'. Upon observing the
action chosen by i, S selects $m_i \in M = \{m_p, m_a\}$, where m_p denotes
'punish' and m_a 'acquiesce'. In period i S prefers that player i obeys,
while if i fails to obey S's preference for punishment or acquiescence
depends on the cost of punishment in period i, which is captured by S's
type at i, t_i; $t_i \in \{0, 1\}$. Thus, other things equal, in period i S prefers to
punish if $t_i = 0$ and prefers to acquiesce if $t_i = 1$.[32] The principal difference in the current model with that in Kreps and Wilson [47] is that
in the latter S's types are known to be the same across periods, i.e.
$t_1 = t_2$, while in the current model S's types are assumed to be independent draws from a Bernoulli distribution with parameter q; thus q is the
true probability punishment will be costly in any one period. S is
assumed to know q, while players 1 and 2 have subjective beliefs about
q summarized by a random variable Q having a Beta distribution with
parameters (α, β). Thus, initially players' 1 and 2 have $E(q) = \alpha/(\alpha + \beta)$ and $\text{var}(q) = \alpha \cdot \beta/(\alpha + \beta)^2(\alpha + \beta + 1))$, and what player 2 is

---

[32] To get this Calvert [24] assumes there is an arbitrarily small benefit for punishing if
$t_i = 0$.

attempting to infer from the period 1 behavior of S is the true value of q.

The time i payoffs for i, S are given by

$$u_i(t_i, m_i, a_i) = \begin{cases} 0 & \text{if } a_i = a_0 \\ b & \text{if } a_i = a_r \text{ and } m_i = m_a, \\ b - 1 & \text{if } a_i = a_r \text{ and } m_i = m_p \end{cases}$$

$$u_s(t_i, m_i, a_i) = \begin{cases} u & \text{if } a_i = a_0 \\ 0 & \text{if } a_i = a_r \text{ and } m_i = m_a, \\ -t_i & \text{if } a_i = a_r \text{ and } m_i = m_p \end{cases}$$

where $u > 1$ and $0 < b < 1$.

A strategy for S then consists of a pair of functions

$$s_i: T \times [0, 1] \to \Delta(M), \quad i = 1, 2,$$

although, as we shall see, we will be able to ignore the dependence of s_i on the parameter q. A strategy for player 1 is simply a probability distribution $r_1 \in \Delta(A)$, while for player 2 a strategy is given by

$$r_2: A \times M \to \Delta(A),$$

with the requirement that $r_2(a_0, m_p) = r_2(a_0, m_a)$, since if player 1 obeys player 2 does not observe a decision by S.

From the specification of the payoffs above we see that at time $i = 2$ S will choose m_p in response to a_r if $t_2 = 0$, and choose m_a if $t_2 = 1$, so in any equilibrium $s_2^*(m_p, 0) = 1$ and $s_2^*(m_a, 1) = 1$. Therefore the payoff to S from player 2 rebelling is the same regardless of t_2, implying that without loss of generality we can ignore the functional dependence of s_2 on the value of q.

Suppose we assume $a_1 = a_r$, i.e. player 1 rebels. Since the behavior of S at $i = 2$ is already determined, the subsequent play of S and player 2 now constitutes a signaling game, where the 'message' sent by S, namely her response to 1 rebelling, does not directly enter player 2's utility function. Any influence of the messages on the behavior of player 2 occurs through the possibility of holding different beliefs about q, i.e. the likelihood t_2 equals zero, following different messages. In particular, suppose following a message player 2 believes that $t_1 = 0$ with probability 1; then by Bayes' Rule the updated Beta distribution over q would have parameters $(\alpha, \beta + 1)$, and player 2 would then respond accordingly. Similarly if 2 believes $t_1 = 1$ the updated Beta would have parameters $(\alpha + 1, \beta)$. Hence if S separates in her first period decision player 2 will revise his beliefs concerning the likelihood that $t_2 = 0$, and hence the likelihood S will punish a rebellion at $i = 2$. On the other hand, if S pools in period i player 2 maintains the prior belief about q associated with the parameters (α, β).

Calvert [24] shows that the unique intuitive equilibrium has the following form, parameterized by the ·value of b: for all values of b $s_1^*(m_p, 0) = 1$, so that S always punishes at $i = 1$ if it is costless. If $b \leq \beta/(\alpha + \beta)$, then $r_1^*(a_0) = r_2^*(a_0, \cdot) = 1$, so both players obey and S is never called upon to punish. If $b \geq (\beta + 1)/(\alpha + \beta + 1)$, then $r_1^*(a_r) = r_1^*(a_r, \cdot) = 1$, and $s_1^*(m_a, 1) = 1$, i.e. player 1 rebels, S punishes in period 1 only if it is costless, and player 2 rebels upon observing either punishment or acquiescence at $i = 1$. In such an equilibrium, then, S separates in her $i = 1$ decision. Upon observing punishment player 2 is certain that $t_1 = 0$; on the other hand this does not imply that t_2 is necessarily equal to 0, since precise knowledge of t_1 does not imply setting q equal to zero or one.· Indeed, in this instance the parameters α, β, and b are such that player 2 prefers to rebel given the prior beliefs, and *still* prefers to rebel even when t_1 is known to be equal to 0. Thus S separates, but such separation is ineffective at influencing player 2's behavior. Finally, if $b \in (\beta/(\alpha + \beta), (\beta + 1)/(\alpha + \beta + 1))$ and $b > (\sigma \cdot \alpha + \beta)/(\alpha + \beta)$, then $r_1^*(a_r) = 1$, $s_1^*(m_p, 1) = \sigma$, and $r_2^*(a_r, m_p) = (u - 1)/u$, $r_2^*(a_r, m_a) = 1$, where

$$\sigma = \frac{\beta \cdot [1 - (b(\alpha + \beta + 1) - \beta)]}{\alpha(b(\alpha + \beta + 1) - \beta)}. \tag{62}$$

Thus player 1 rebels; if $t_1 = 0$ S punishes with certainty, and if $t_1 = 1$ S punishes with probability σ, where σ is such that upon observing punishment player 2's updated belief concerning q renders 2 indifferent between obeying and rebelling. Player 2 then randomizes in such a fashion as to render S indifferent between punishing and acquiescing at $i = 1$ if $t_1 = 1$. In this instance with positive probability player 2 is deterred from rebelling when according to the prior belief he would prefer to rebel, while player 1 always rebels. Finally, if player 2 observes $m_1 = m_a$ he rebels with certainty. The remaining case is where $b \in (\beta/(\alpha + \beta), (\sigma \cdot \alpha + \beta)/(\alpha + \beta))$; in this instance $r_1^*(a_0) = 1 = r_2^*(a_r, \cdot)$, where such behavior by player 1 is optimal given $s_1^*(\cdot)$ is as described in the previous case. Therefore player 1 is deterred from rebelling, but not player 2.

Summarizing, we see that for relatively low values of b players always obey, where such behavior is optimal given the prior belief about q. In particular, whenever the players would obey in the one-shot game (i.e. $b \leq \beta/(\alpha + \beta)$) they obey in the 'two-shot' game as well. On the other hand for relatively high values of b rebellion always occurs even when S reveals himself to be a 'punisher' at $i = 1$. Finally, for intermediate values of b deterrence is effective, in that the behavior of S at $i = 1$ keeps one or the other player from rebelling, while in the one-shot game the players would rebel. In particular, S punishes with positive probability at $i = 1$, even when such punishment is costly, to provide the incentive for one of the players to obey when otherwise they would have rebelled. This lack of rebellion then justifies S bearing the cost of punishment at $i = 1$.

Thus we see how reputation building and costly punishment persist as equilibrium phenomena. For some values of the parameters the political leader in Calvert [24] or the hegemon in Alt, Calvert, and Humes [2] prefers to incur the positive cost of punishing current transgressions, since such behavior enhances the belief about the likelihood of future punishments and thereby mitigates the possibility of further transgressions. In this manner stability within a collective is maintained and the goals of its leadership advanced through the initial wielding of a 'big stick' by the leadership onto the backsides of uncooperative associates.

7. CRISIS BARGAINING

7.1. Introduction

Much of what political scientists think of as the study of international relations has to do with the outbreak of war and the negotiations over contested issues through which the interested parties attempt to avoid war, where war is typically modeled as a socially inferior outcome. In this section we examine recent papers dealing with such bargaining in the shadow of war, wherein the parties (assumed to number two) have the ability to resolve the issue short of war, and where the presence of incomplete information complicates the willingness and ability of the parties to do so.

In one series of papers, war can be thought of as a cataclysmic nuclear exchange, and hence 'unwinnable,' where the probability of such an exchange is set exogenously and is assumed to increase over time. We can think of this probability as an autonomous risk of war which grows due to an increasing likelihood of the process spiraling out of control as the bargaining continues. We examine in detail the model of Powell [65], in which uncertainty surrounds the critical risk level of one of the parties such that this party would prefer to accept the opponent's demands rather than continue the process even when the opponent would 'give in' at the next instance; this level is known as the player's *resolve*. Powell [65] then shows how uncertainty about an opponent's resolve can lead to the outbreak of a nuclear exchange, and he also derives characteristics of successful or unsuccessful bargaining prior to an exchange.[33]

In another series of papers, war results from the conscious decisions of the bargainers, where in particular the outcome from a war is in some instances preferred to giving in to an opponent's demands. In Morrow [55] the payoffs from war are a function of both parties' military capabilities. If one party is relatively 'strong' and the other 'weak', the former has a higher probability of winning the war and achieving its desired outcome on the disputed issue, albeit at some cost from fighting the war. Uncertainty about the opponent's military capability then presents the opportunity for inferring this information through the opponent's decisions in the bargaining process. If no demand has been accepted after some finite time, a war begins.[34]

In both models the bargaining process is such that war would never be an equilibrium outcome if information were complete; hence incomplete information is necessary for war to occur.[35] This conclusion, while a generally accepted wisdom prior to the development of these

---

[33] See also Nalebuff [62]. Powell [66] extends his earlier work by assuming two-sided incomplete information where both players' resolve is private information, and Powell [67] alters the strategic set-up of the original game by replacing the 'escalation' moves with acts of limited warfare which drain the opponent's resources.

[34] Morrow [56] studies this bargaining process in a repeated framework, and Morrow [57] examines the strategy of 'linking' issues together in the bargaining process. Bueno de Mesquita and Lalman [22] study a model similar to Morrow [55] in which types refer to levels of domestic opposition to fighting a war, and Wagner [80] models the Cuban missile crisis as a bargaining game with incomplete information.

[35] This is not to say that it is not possile to write down a complete information sequential move (hence perfect information) game where war is an equilibrium outcome; see Bueno de Mesquite and Lalman [21]. However applying the Rubinstein [74] result to the current situation suggests that in any 'alternating offer' type of bargaining war will not occur under complete information.

models (cf. Snyder and Diesing [77], Wagner [79]), has not deterred previous research from focusing on complete information environments since, as noted in Section 1, the theory of incomplete information games is of a fairly recent vintage. The current models then begin the process of re-working the analysis of crisis bargaining and war with a set of tools, namely incomplete information games, that is consistent with commonly held beliefs about the environment within which such crises arise.

7.2. Escalation to an unwinnable war

The model of Powell [65] involves a crisis bargaining game among two players, S and R, with four possible outcomes: the status quo, x_0, a resolution favoring S, x_s, a resolution favoring R, x_r, and all-out war, x_w. Player j's ordinal preferences over the outcomes in $X = \{x_0, x_s, x_r, x_w\}$, denoted $>_j$, satisfy $x_j >_j x_0 >_j x_k >_j x_w, j, k = S, R, j \neq k$. Hence neither side wants to go to war, and both sides prefer resolution in their favor to the status quo. Uncertainty is introduced by assuming S's cardinal utility for the outcome x_s can take on one of two values; let $t \in T = \{t_1, t_2\}$ parameterize these values, and let $p \in (0, 1)$ denote the prior probability S is of type t_1.

The sequence of actions and events are as follows: initially R decides whether to initiate a crisis or accept the status quo: if R initiates, S has the option to submit to R's 'demands', m_r, thereby generating the outcome x_r, begin a war, m_w, generating the outcome x_w, or escalate the crisis, m_e. If S escalates, 'nature' begins a war with probability g, where $g > 0$ and for technical reasons $6 \cdot g < 1$. If S escalates and nature does not begin a war, then R can either submit to S, a_s, thereby generating x_s, escalate, a_e, or begin a war, a_w. If R escalates, then with probability $2 \cdot g$ nature begins a war, and if no war occurs then again it is S's turn to move, where following another escalation of the crisis nature begins a war with probability $3 \cdot g$, etc.

Thus the game ends when either S submits to R's demands, R submits to S's demands, or a war begins, either through choice or by a move by nature. We can think of these moves by nature as capturing an autonomous risk of war derived by the continuation of the crisis, where the likelihood the process will spiral out of control and into a war increases the longer the crisis persists. Clearly neither player would ever choose to attack the opponent as long as the autonomous risk of war at the next instance is less than one, so without loss of generality we can ignore this choice by the players. Hence neither player will consciously choose to start a war at any time, yet their continued persistence in the bargaining makes the outbreak of war more likely.

Although this crisis could in principle continue for quite some time, Powell [65] renders the analysis tractable by assuming that if R has escalated the crisis and war has not occurred, then S's payoffs are such that if S is of type t_1 she will prefer to accept R's demands rather than escalate even if R would accept S's demands at the next opportunity, whereas given the same scenario if S is of type t_2 she would prefer to escalate. In particular, define the *resolve* of S of type t_i as

$$\rho_s(t_i) = \frac{u_s(x_s, t_i) - u_s(x_r)}{u_s(x_s, t_i) - u_s(x_w)}. \tag{63}$$

Thus the resolve of S if type t_i is the probability of war which makes t_i indifferent between accepting R's demands and escalating the crisis given that R will at his next move accept S's demands; similarly we can define the resolve of R as ρ_r. The assumption in Powell [65] then is that

$$g < \rho_s(t_1) < 3 \cdot g < \rho_s(t_2) < 5 \cdot g, \text{ and} \tag{64}$$

$$2 \cdot g < \rho_r < 4 \cdot g. \tag{65}$$

Thus if R knew that S is of type t_1, following m_e R would prefer to escalate, since S will certainly submit at the next decision, whereas if R knew that $t = t_2$ R would prefer to submit, since S will escalate knowing that R would subsequently submit. Hence the payoffs to S and R following an escalation by R are completely determined by S's type. Conditional on R initiating a crisis, the game reduces to a signaling game between S and R where $M = \{m_r, m_e\}$, $A = \{a_s, a_e\}$, and the payoffs can be written as functions of $u_s(\cdot)$, $u_r(\cdot)$, t, and g. A strategy for S then is as before, $s: T \to \Delta(M)$, and, since the message m_r ends the game, a strategy for R is simply a probability $r(a_e)$ of escalating following an escalation by S.

Clearly there will not exist a separating equilibrium in this game, for if e.g. $s(m_r, t_1) = 1$ and $s(m_e, t_2) = 1$ then upon observing escalation R would know the senders' type to be t_2, and therefore would submit to S; but then S of type t_1 would rather switch and escalate, since $g < \rho_s(t_1)$. Suppose on the other hand $s(m_e, t_1) = s(m_e, t_2) = 1$, so the sender pools at m_e; if $r(a_e) = 1$ then S of type t_1 will subsequently submit to R, implying S would be better off sending m_r, thereby submitting to R's demands with a lower probability of war. If the sender pools at m_e and p is such that the optimal response is $r(a_e) = 0$, then R would never have initiated the crisis in the first place, since the status quo outcome is preferred by R to x_s. Finally, S pooling at m_r cannot be an equilibrium, since S of type t_2 is better off escalating regardless of R's response. Thus Powell [65] shows that the game has a unique sequential equilibrium, with the following path: if $p > p^*$, where $p^* \in (0, 1)$, R does not initiate a crisis, while if $p < p^*$ the equilibrium strategies are $s^*(m_r, t_1) \in (0, 1)$, $s^*(m_e, t_2) = 1$, and $r^*(a_e) \in (0, 1)$. Therefore if it is sufficiently likely *ex ante* that the sender is 'strong', i.e. of type t_2, then R simply accepts the status quo outcome. Otherwise R initiates a crisis, a strong sender always escalates, while a weak sender escalates with positive probability less than one. Upon observing an escalation by S, R is (according to the prior p and s^*) indifferent between escalating and submitting, and escalates with positive probability less than one as well.

Given the behavioral prediction, then, Powell [65] derives the following conclusions: 1) the *ex ante* probability of war occurring is strictly positive and increasing for $p < p^*$. Therefore the probability of war is not monotonic in p, but rather peaks at a strictly interior point. This conclusion clearly differs from that derived from the complete information version of the game, where the probability of war is always zero. 2) With positive probability the state with the *least* resolve prevails; in particular if $t = t_1$ then with probability $s \cdot (1 - r^*(a_e)) \cdot (1 - g)$ S escalates, no war occurs, and R submits. Again, with complete information this never occurs.[36] 3) R is *more likely* to escalate the *greater* is the resolve of the weak sender, $\rho_s(t_1)$; this follows from the algebra of the receiver's mixed strategy necessary to make S of type t_1 indifferent between escalating and submitting.

In this manner Powell [65] shows how an incomplete information environment can explain the occurrence of crisis bargaining and war as an equilibrium phenomenon, thereby justifying formally the informal conclusions of previous authors. However he also shows that the presence of incomplete information in crisis bargaining generates new and somewhat counterintuitive results concerning the behavior of the participants and the likelihood of war.

---

[36] This isn't quite right given the discrete nature of the bidding process. Powell [65] proves this result for the player with the greatest 'effective' resolve, defined as the player willing to make the last bid.

7.3. Bargaining and a winnable war

Morrow [55] examines a model of crisis bargaining where, unlike Powell [65], a war outcome is in equilibrium initiated through the choices of the players. Thus, although war remains socially suboptimal, a player may prefer to go to war rather than accept the current demand of the opponent. As in Powell [65] there exist basically four possible outcomes in the game: the status quo, x_0, a resolution short of war favoring player j, $j = 1, 2$, and war, x_w. Incomplete information is present in that the result of the war, and hence the payoffs of the players attached to the outcome x_w, is a function of the players' types, t_1, t_2, and 'nature's' type t_n, where $t_j \in T = \{0, 1\}$, $j = 1, 2, n$. The players know their own type, but not that of their opponent nor of nature, and the result of a war is a function of the vector (t_1, t_2, t_n) in that if a majority of the values are 1's then 1 'wins' the war, and the resulting payoffs for 1 and 2 are those associated with x_1 less some positive costs of fighting the war; if on the other hand a majority of the values are 0's then 2 wins and the payoffs are those associated with x_2 less the same costs. Let p_j be the *ex ante* probability $t_j = 1$, $j = 1, 2, n$, and set $p_n = 1/2$.

At the beginning of play neither player knows with certainty the payoffs resulting from the war outcome, although each will possess some partial and differential information. In particular, if e.g. $t_1 = 1$, then 1 knows that if either t_2 or t_n equals 1 player 1 will win the war; thus if $t_1 = 1$ we will say that player 1 holds an *advantage*, with a similar definition for player 2 if $t_2 = 0$. On the other hand if $t_1 = 0$ player 1 needs both t_2 and t_n to equal 1 to prevail. Any information concerning the opponent's type revealed through the course of play is thus potentially valuable in the determination of the player's optimal decisions at the bargaining stage.

The sequence of decisions and events is as follows: initially player 1 either begins the crisis, or accepts the status quo, where if 1 initiates he chooses one of three demands, associated with the outcomes x_1, x_0, and x_2. Player 2 can then either accept the demand by player 1, which terminates the game, or make a counterdemand of either x_1, x_0, or x_2. Following a counterdemand player 1 can either accept or make another demand, where this time rejection by player 1 of the current demand begins the war with both sides incurring some initial war costs. After 1's second demand is made, t_n is revealed and player 2 can either continue the war or accept 1's latest demand. If 2 continues the war then the remainder of the war costs are borne and the winner is determined by the vector of types as discussed above.

Morrow [55] parameterizes the intuitive sequential equilibria of his model by the prior beliefs p_1 and p_2, where the definition of 'intuitive beliefs' from Section 2.4 is easily extended to the current non-signaling game structure. As with the model of Powell [65] examined above, for some values of the priors, namely relatively high p_2, player 1 does not initiate a crisis, since it is quite likely player 2 holds an advantage. Otherwise player 1 initiates a crisis regardless of type, and the typical equilibrium scenario has the following path: at each turn player j rejects the current demand and makes a counterdemand if j holds an advantage, and accepts the current demand with positive probability less than one if j does not hold an advantage. Therefore with positive probability the bargaining is successfully concluded prior to war occurring, with each side at times prevailing in the outcome. Further, the strategies are such that as demands are rejected and the bargaining continues each player places greater probability on the opponent holding an advantage. However in spite of this the probability of a war occurring remains strictly positive even though war is sub-optimal and information is being transmitted through the players' behavior. The key to this result is that, as in Powell [65], the equilibrium involves 'noisy' signaling; if the equilibrium strategies separated types early in the bargaining process, then war could be averted. Yet such separation by the players is inconsistent with equilibrium play: weak types, i.e. those not holding an advantage, would always prefer to mimic the behavior of strong types.

Thus Morrow [55] rationalizes the outbreak of winnable but sub-optimal wars as an equilibrium phenomenon. In addition, Morrow [55] shows that war is more likely to occur the greater is the *ex ante* probability that each side holds an advantage up to the critical value of p_2 where player 1 prefers to not initiate a crisis in the first place, a conclusion analogous to that derived in Powell [65]. Finally, Morrow [55] identifies the presence of a selection bias with respect to the occurrence of crises and wars, in that not all specifications of the parameters, in particular the prior beliefs, lead inexorably to war. Thus the mere fact of a crisis or war occurring implies the relevant parameters are not random but rather must satisfy the conditions generated by the model for a crisis to persist.[37]

---

[37] Banks [15] shows this selection bias to be a general feature of crisis bargaining games; that is, it exists regardless of the extensive form of the game.

8. VOTING WITH INCOMPLETE INFORMATION

8.1. Introduction

The final substantive topic we examine concerns optimal voting behavior by individuals faced with a binary voting agenda, from which a single alternative is to be chosen. Suppose we have a finite set of alternatives X and of voters N, $|N|$ odd, where each voter possesses a strict preference order on the set X. Let the voters determine an outcome from X by employing a binary voting tree of finite length where at each stage voters simultaneously and by majority rule decide whether to proceed 'left' or 'right', and where there exists a function mapping alternatives in X to terminal nodes of the tree; assume that all $x \in X$ are associated with at least one such terminal node. Then if the preferences of all voters are common knowledge, the unique (perfect) equilibrium outcome is easily determined by backward induction: at all penultimate nodes, i.e. those followed only by terminal nodes, each voter has an incentive to vote 'sincerely' between the alternatives associated with going left or right. Hence by complete information all voters can solve for the outcome upon reaching any penultimate node, thereby inducing preferences over going left or right at the nodes immediately preceding the penultimate nodes, and so each voter can solve for the resulting outcome upon reaching these nodes, and so on.[38] A straightforward prediction of such a game then is that, if there exists a Condorcet alternative, i.e. an alternative which is majority-preferred to all others, then regardless of the binary voting procedure this alternative is chosen as the equilibrium outcome (McKelvey and Niemi [51]).

On the other hand Ordeshook and Palfrey [64] demonstrate the difficulties with reaching such a conclusion in the presence of incomplete information concerning the voters' preferences. They consider an environment with three alternatives and three voters, where the voting tree constitutes an 'amendment procedure': initially two alternatives are put to a vote, with the winner then going up against the remaining alternative; the winning alternative at this second stage is then declared the outcome. At the second stage voters will continue to behave sincerely; however the optimal behavior of the voters at the first stage

---

[38] See McKelvey and Niemi [51]. This process is analogous in this situation to applying Moulin's [59] dominance solvability.

will be a function of their beliefs about the others' types, i.e. preferences. Although different types may behave differently at the first stage, and hence signal their information to the others, such information is not valuable in that the optimal second stage behavior of all voters is simply to vote for their preferred alternative. Therefore the key substantive issues in Ordeshook and Palfrey [65] concern not the informativeness of the first stage voting choices, but rather the general effect of incomplete information on the equilibrium predictions about voting behavior.

In contrast, Jung [44] considers voting behavior with incomplete information under variants of a 'successive procedure': voters initially vote on whether to select $x \in X$ as the outcome; if x is not selected then it is no longer a possible outcome, and the voters proceed to vote on whether to select alternative $y \in X$ as the outcome or not, etc., where if all but one alternative has been rejected the remaining alternative is then the outcome. Jung [44] shows that the results of Ordeshook and Palfrey [64] do not extend to the successive procedure under a particular assumption about preferences and the order in which the alternatives are considered.

8.2. The amendment procedure and a negative result

Consider a committee of three voters, $N = \{1, 2, 3\}$, and three alternatives, $X = \{x, y, z\}$, where the committee selects an outcome from X using an 'amendment procedure' wherein at stage 1 the voters vote for either x or y, and then at stage 2 for the winner from stage 1 or z. Voting at each stage is simultaneous, and for simplicity assume that prior to stage 2 the voters only know the winner from stage 1, rather than the votes by each member of the committee (this assumption will be justified below). The voters' preferences over X are a function of their types, where each voter can either be type t_x, thereby preferring x to y to z, type t_y, who prefers y to z to x, or type t_z, who prefers z to x to y; let the utility payoff to a voter's most/middle/least preferred alternative be $1/u/0$, respectively, where $u \in (0, 1)$, and let $T = \{t_x, t_y, t_z\}$. Voters' types are assumed to be independent and identically distributed according to the prior $p = (p_x, p_y, p_z)$. Given this structure then a (pure) strategy for voter i is a set of decision rules $v_i = (v_i^1, v_i^2)$, where

$$v_i^1: T \to \{x, y\}$$
$$v_i^2: T \times \{j\} \to \{j, z\}, j = x, y.$$

A (Bayesian) equilibrium then is a profile of decision rules $v^* = (v_1^*, v_2^*, v_3^*)$ such that v_i is optimal given v_{-i}^* for $i = 1, 2, 3$.

Ordeshook and Palfrey [64] focus on symmetric equilibria of the above game, so that without loss of generality we can drop the subscript on voters' strategies. In addition they require the strategies to be undominated, implying that at each stage voters condition their decision on being pivotal, i.e. on the remaining voters splitting their votes between the two alternatives considered. Weak dominance then implies that in equilibrium all voters vote 'sincerely' at stage 2: $v^2(t_x, x) = x$, $v^2(t_y, x) = v^2(t_z, y) = z$, and $v^2(t_x, y) = v^2(t_y, y) = y$, $v^2(t_z, y) = z$. Thus our earlier assumption concerning the observed variables from the stage 1 decisions was without loss of generality; as in the Austen-Smith [4] model without debate, any information about voters' types revealed through the stage 1 decisions arrives too late to affect the optimality of the stage 2 decisions non-trivially. In particular, with three alternatives and no debate, there does not exist the possibility of signaling influential information through the stage 1 votes. Weak dominance also implies that a voter of type t_y will vote sincerely at stage 1, since this type (weakly) prefers *any* lottery over alternatives $\{y, z\}$ to *all* lotteries over $\{x, z\}$; this in turn implies that in equilibrium type t_z voters vote sincerely at stage 1 as well. It remains to determine the equilibrium choice of a type t_x voter at stage 1.

Note that with complete information and exactly 1 voter of each type, the (unique) equilibrium behavior of types t_y and t_z is the same as above, namely they vote sincerely at each stage. This follows since now it is evident to the voters that if alternative x prevails at stage 1 the final outcome will be z, while if y prevails y will be the final outcome. Hence the choice at stage 1 is in reality between generating z or y as the final outcome, and type t_y voters prefer outcome y and hence vote for y, while type t_z voters prefer z and hence vote for x, which coincides with a 'sincere' choice of x over y. On the other hand with complete information type t_x voters prefer to vote 'insincerely' for y over x, since they prefer the outcome induced by y to that induced by x. Hence, as in the environment with incomplete information, the issue of sincere versus insincere voting focuses on the decision by the type t_x voters at stage 1.

Ordeshook and Palfrey [64] show that if $p_1/(p_1 + p_3) > u$ then $v^1(t_x) = x$, along with the decision rules described above, constitutes an equilibrium. Thus if the *ex ante* probability of type t_x occurring is high relative to the probability of t_z, all voters voting sincerely is an equilibrium. The logic of this result is that, given the conjecture that all voters are sincere, a type t_x voter realizes that if he is pivotal at stage 1 the voter voting for y at stage 1 must be type t_y, so that the remaining voter is either t_x or t_z. If the voter believed this remaining voter was t_x then he should vote for x, thereby generating x as the final outcome since there would exist two type t_x voters. On the other hand, if he believed the remaining voter is t_z he should vote for y, since the t_z voter and the t_y voter would constitute a majority and thereby implement z if x was chosen at stage 1. In general then the optimal decision rule for t_x at stage 1 will depend on the relative likelihood the remaining voter is t_x rather than t_z. Alternatively, if $p_1/(p_1 + p_2) < u$ then $v^1(x_z) = y$ is an equilibrium, where this follows from a similar logic. Therefore it is possible to have 1) a unique symmetric equilibrium where all voters vote sincerely, 2) a unique symmetric equilibrium where only type t_x voters vote insincerely, 3) both of these equilibria existing simultaneously, or 4) no (pure strategy) symmetric equilibria.

Ordeshook and Palfrey [64] then go on to show that the existence of these 'insincere' equilibria renders the efficacy of the majority rule amendment procedure problematic in the presence of incomplete information. Suppose the above environment is generalized to one with n voters, n odd, where again all voters are either type t_x, t_y, or t_z. Then the behavior of types t_y and t_z is unchanged from that above, while the relevant critical values for type t_x voters are now as follows: if

$$[p_1/(p_1 + p_3)]^{(n-1)/2} > u, \qquad (66)$$

then $v^1(t_x) = x$ is an equilibrium, while if

$$[p_1/(p_1 + p_2)]^{(n-1)/2} < u \qquad (67)$$

$v^1(t_z) = y$ is an equilibrium. In particular, for any values of the parameters p, u, if n is sufficiently large eq. (67) will hold while eq. (66) will not, implying the only symmetric equilibrium is one in which type t_x voters are insincere. Therefore, even if p_1 is close to 1, implying alternative x is almost certainly a Condorcet winner, x is never selected if the committee is large enough. This result contrasts with the result under complete information noted in Section 8.1 that if a Condorcet winner exists then it is the unique equilibrium outcome. Hence the presence of incomplete information concerning voter preferences can radically alter the 'welfare' properties of majority voting under the amendment procedure.[39]

8.3. The successive procedure and a positive result

Ordeshook and Palfrey [64] note that their negative result concerning the amendment procedure is not a function of assuming the presence of only three of the six possible preferences orderings, the 'middle' value u being equal across voters, the presence of only three alternatives, or the use of the amendment procedure. However Jung [44] shows that this conclusion is not completely general by constructing a binary voting procedure which, together with an assumption on the allowable types of preferences, implements with certainty the Condorcet alternative. Suppose we have n voters, with m alternatives $X = \{x_1, \ldots, x_m\}$ aligned on the real line. Label X such that $x_1 < \ldots < x_m$, and suppose the set of voter types is restricted to preferences orders which are 'single-peaked' over X. The assumption of single-peaked preferences then guarantees that a complete information Condorcet winner exists, and the goal is to construct a procedure which provides the incentive for 'sincere' behavior, thereby generating the Condorcet winner as the equilibrium outcome. Consider the following binary procedure for selecting an outcome from X: at the first stage the voters vote whether to make x_1 the outcome or not; if not, they proceed to stage 2 and vote whether to make x_2 the outcome or not, etc.; if $m - 1$ negative votes have occurred, the final outcome is set at x_m. Then Jung [44] shows that regardless of the prior beliefs, the scaling of utilities, etc., the unique equilibrium is the complete information Condorcet winner. In fact, Jung [44] characterizes a class of binary procedures, all of which implement the Condorcet winner. This result holds even though with more than three alternatives there exists the possibility of transmitting valuable information to other voters in the early stages of the voting, implying some types of voters may attempt to pool with other types in order to achieve a preferable outcome. However it turns out that in the procedure Jung [44] analyzes the equilibrium decision by each type of voter is not a function of their beliefs concerning others' types (other than their existence).

---

[39] Of course, another conclusion from eqs. (66) and (67) is that for any values of u and n, if p_1 is sufficiently close to 1 the only symmetric equilibrium is sincere.

The key to Jung's result is that at each stage of the voting process the set of possible outcomes is partitioned into two subsets, each of which are 'connected' relative to the ordering of alternatives in X along the real line. With single peaked preferences, then, at each stage all types either have a dominant strategy to vote one way or the other, or else can solve for an optimal strategy conditional on the former types using their dominant strategies. For the former types the partition will 'separate' their preferences, in that the least preferred alternative in one set is preferred to the most preferred alternative in the complementary set. For example, if $m = 3$, then there are 4 possible single peaked orderings; $t_1: x_1 > x_2 > x_3$; $t_2: x_2 > x_1 > x_3$; $t_3: x_2 > x_3 > x_1$; and $t_4: x_3 > x_2 > x_1$. Thus, if x_1 is considered initially, voters of type t_1 have a dominant strategy of voting for x_1, while types t_3 and t_4 have a dominant strategy of voting against x_1, since they prefer any lottery of x_2 and x_3 to x_1.[40] Voters of type t_2 do not have a dominant strategy; however given the presumed behavior of other types and conditional on being pivotal at stage 1, t_2 types should vote against x_1 as well. This follows because, at the next stage, types t_1, t_2, and t_3 will vote for x_2, while t_4 types will vote against x_2; therefore if a t_2 voter is decisive at stage 1, there cannot exist a majority of t_4 voters, implying x_2 will be the outcome if t_2 votes against x_1.

Therefore the only types that vote for x_1 at the first stage are types t_1, implying x_1 is the final outcome only if there exists a majority of type t_1 voters, i.e. if x_1 is the complete information Condorcet winner. Similarly x_3 is the resulting outcome if types t_4 are in the majority, and x_2 is the outcome if types t_2 together with t_3 constitute a majority. Therefore the unique equilibrium outcome will coincide with the complete information Condorcet winning alternative. Now suppose we add a fourth alternative, x_4, where $x_4 > x_3$, and where x_4 is considered first. Then the previous arguments determine the behavior if x_4 is rejected, and again one can show that the only types that will vote for x_4 at stage 1 are those that have x_4 as their most preferred alternative. Thus x_4 will only be selected if a majority of voters are of this type, i.e. if x_4 is a Condorcet winner. In this manner then Jung [40] is able to show that this successive elimination procedure (Bayesian) implements the Condorcet winning alternative.

---

[40] Recall that all voters will behave sincerely at the second stage in voting for or against x_2, where the latter generates x_3 as the outcome.

In general, equilibrium voting under incomplete information can be quite sensitive to the assumptions concerning the preferences of the voters and the process involved in selecting an outcome. Whereas some procedures provide the incentive for the voters to act sincerely, other commonly used procedures such as the amendment procedure can be quite sensitive to the underlying parameters and the structure of voting.

9. DISCUSSION

This monograph has explored the effects of incomplete information on models of political interactions. We have seen how the presence of informational asymmetries assists in explaining observed phenomena such as wars, debate, reputation-building, and the use of restrictive rules as the outcomes from the decisions of rational, optimizing actors. In addition, we have seen how the manifestations of these asymmetries differ according to the social environment under scrutiny: in certain environments all available information is revealed through the actors' choices, where these choices at times exhibit a bias owing to the incentive costs of such revelation, whereas in others only a limited amount of information can be transmitted. Further, the content of the information transmitted might in some circumstances be useless with regard to the decision calculus of the actors.

Still, what is also clear from examining the models presented in this monograph is that the use of incomplete information games in political science is in a fairly embryonic stage of development in terms of both the substantive issues addressed and the appropriateness of the game forms analyzed. There exists numerous other topics concerning voting and legislative behavior, coalition formation, etc., in which the assumption of incomplete information may be both reasonable and insightful.[41] Additional areas of research include the effects of regulation and political institutions on primarily economic variables such as market entry, mergers, and monetary policy.[42]

---

[41] Recent additions to this literature include Austen-Smith [6] on an incumbent's ability to explain her legislative behavior to her constituency, and Austen-Smith and Wright [10] on lobbyists competing for the votes of a legislator.

[42] On this last topic some work already exists: Rogoff and Sibert [70] and Alesina and Cukierman [1] model decisions on macroeconomic policy variables as arising from the electoral competition of candidates in which one or both possess private information.

From a methodological viewpoint the models we have examined are quite simple descriptions of the interactions of the actors. One dimension of this simplicity is the 'one-shot' nature of the interaction; for example, a more natural or realistic model of the committee-floor decisions would be one in which these actors interact repeatedly over time, where the private information and the previous decisions effect the relevant parameters at any one time. However while it is evident that such dynamic models would be preferable in understanding the influence of incomplete information on the strategic interaction of political agents, it is also evident that the models examined in this monograph have already established important results in this regard, at the same time creating a foundation on which to build additional and more sophisticated models of political behavior.

REFERENCES

[1]   Alesina, Alberto, and Alex Cukierman, 'The Politics of Ambiguity', working paper, Hoover Institution, 1988.

[2]   Alt, James, Randall Calvert, and Brian Humes, 'Reputation and Hegemonic Stability: A Game-Theoretic Analysis,' *American Political Science Review* **82** (1988), 445–466.

[3]   Aumann, Robert, 'Agreeing to Disagree,' *Annals of Statistics* **4** (1976), 1236–1239.

[4]   Austen-Smith, David, 'Credible Debate Equilibria,' *Social Choice and Welfare* **7** (1990), 75–93.

[5]   Austen-Smith, David, 'Information Transmission in Debate,' *American Journal of Political Science* **34** (1990), 124–152.

[6]   Austen-Smith, David, 'Explaining the Vote,' manuscript, University of Rochester, 1989.

[7]   Austen-Smith, David, and Jeffrey Banks, 'Electoral Accountability and Incumbency,' in *Models of Strategic Choice in Politics*, ed. by Peter Ordeshook. Ann Arbor: University of Michigan Press, 1989.

[8]   Austen-Smith, David, and William Riker, 'Asymmetric Information and the Coherence of Legislation,' *American Political Science Review* **81** (1987), 897–918.

[9]   Austen-Smith, David, and William Riker, 'Asymmetric Information and the Coherence of Legislation: Correction,' *American Political Science Review* **84** (1990), 243–248.

[10] Austen-Smith, David, and John Wright, 'Competitive Lobbying for Legislators' Votes,' manuscript, University of Rochester, 1989.

[11] Bain, Joseph, 'A Note on Pricing in Monopoly and Oligopoly,' *American Economic Review* **39** (1949), 448–464.

[12] Banks, Jeffrey, 'Agency Budgets, Cost Information, and Auditing,' *American Journal of Political Science* **33** (1989) 670–699.

[13] Banks, Jeffrey, 'Monopoly Agenda Control with Asymmetric Information,' *Quarterly Journal of Economics* **105** (1990), 445–464.

[14] Banks, Jeffrey, 'A Model of Electoral Competition with Incomplete Information,' *Journal of Economic Theory* **50** (1990), 309–325.

[15] Banks, Jeffrey, 'Equilibrium Behavior in Crisis Bargaining Games,' *American Journal of Political Science* **34** (1990), 599–614.

[16] Banks, Jeffrey, 'Regulatory Auditing without Commitment,' manuscript, University of Rochester, 1989.

[17] Banks, Jeffrey, 'Monopoly Agenda Control with Two-Sided Uncertainty,' manuscript, University of Rochester, 1989.

[18] Banks, Jeffrey, and Joel Sobel, 'Equilibrium Selection in Signaling Games,' *Econometrica* **55** (1987), 647–661.

[19] Banks, Jeffrey, and Joel Sobel, 'Equilibrium Selection in Signaling Games,' Caltech working paper no. 565, 1985.

[20] Bendor, Jonathan, Serge Taylor, and Roland Van Gaalen, 'Politicians, Bureaucrats, and Asymmetric Information,' *American Journal of Political Science* **31** (1987), 796–828.

[21] Bueno de Mesquita, Bruce, and David Lalman, 'The Road to War is Strewn with Peaceful Intentions', in *Models of Strategic Choice in Politics*, ed. by Peter Ordeshook. Ann Arbor: University of Michigan Press, 1989.

[22] Bueno de Mesquita, Bruce, and David Lalman, 'Domestic Opposition and Foreign War,' *American Political Science Review* **84** (1990), 747–766.

[23] Calvert, Randall, *Models of Imperfect Information in Politics*. Fundamentals of Pure and Applied Economics, Chur: Harwood Academic Publishers, 1986.

[24] Calvert, Randall, 'Reputation and Legislative Leadership,' *Public Choice* **55** (1987), 81–119.

[25] Cho, In-Koo, and David Kreps, 'Signaling Games and Stable Equilibria,' *Quarterly Journal of Economics* **102** (1987) 179–221.

[26] Cho, In-Koo, and Joel Sobel, 'Strategic Stability and Uniqueness in Signaling Games,' *Journal of Economic Theory* **50** (1990), 381–413.

[27] Cooper, Joseph, *The Origins of the Standing Committees and the Development of the Modern House*. Houston: Rice University Studies.

[28] Crawford, Vincent, and Joel Sobel, 'Strategic Information Transmission,' *Econometrica* **50** (1982) 1431–1451.

[29] d'Aspremont, Claude, and Louis-Andre Gerard-Varet, 'Incentives and Incomplete Information,' *Journal of Public Economics* **11** (1979) 25–45.

[30] Denzau, Arthur, and Robert Mackay, 'Gatekeeping and Monopoly Power of Committees: An Analysis of Sincere and Sophisticated Behavior,' *American Journal of Political Science* **27** (1983) 740–761.

[31] Downs, Anthony, *An Economic Theory of Democracy*. New York: Harper and Row, 1957.

[32] Farrell, Joseph, 'Cheap Talk, Coordination, and Entry,' *Rand Journal of Economics* **18** (1987), 34–39.

[33] Farrell, Joseph, 'Credible Neologisms in Games of Communication,' MIT working paper, 1984.

[34] Ferejohn, John, 'Incumbent Performance and Electoral Control,' *Public Choice* **50** (1986), 5–25.

[35] Friedman, James, 'On Entry Preventing Behavior,' in *Applied Game Theory*, ed. by Steven Brams, *et al.* Vienna: Physica-Verlag, 1979, pp. 236–253.

[36] Gilligan, Thomas, and Keith Krehbiel, 'Collective Decision-Making and Standing Committees: An Informational Rationale for Restrictive Amendment Procedures,' *Journal of Law, Economics, and Organization* **3** (1987), 287–335.

[37] Gilligan, Thomas, and Keith Krehbiel, 'Asymmetric Information and Legislative Rules with a Heterogeneous Committee,' *American Journal of Political Science* **33** (1989) 459–490.

[38] Gilligan, Thomas, and Keith Krehbiel, 'Collective Choice without Procedural Commitment,' in *Strategic Models of Politics*, ed. by Peter Ordeshook. Ann Arbor: University of Michigan Press, 1989.

[39] Grossman, Sanford, and Motty Perry, 'Perfect Sequential Equilibria,' *Journal of Economic Theory* **39** (1986), 97–119.

[40] Harrington, Joseph, 'The Revelation of Information through the Electoral Process,' manuscript, Johns Hopkins University, 1988.

[41] Harsanyi, John, 'Games with Incomplete Information Played by Bayesian Players,' *Management Science* **14** (1967-8), 159–182, 320–334, 486–502.

[42] Harsanyi, John, *Rational Behavior and Bargaining Equilibrium in Games and Social Situations*. London: Cambridge University Press, 1977.

[43] Hotelling, Harold, 'Stability in Competition,' *Economic Journal* **39** (1929), 41–57.

[44] Jung, Joon Pyo, 'Condorcet Consistent Binary Agendas under Incomplete Information,' in *Models of Strategic Choice in Politics*, ed. by Peter Ordeshook. Ann Arbor: Michigan University Press, 1989.

[45] Kohlberg, Elon, and Jean-Francois Mertens, 'On the Strategic Stability of Equilibria,' *Econometrica* **54** (1986), 1003–1037.

[46] Kreps, David, and Robert Wilson, 'Sequential Equilibria,' *Econometrica* **50** (1982), 863–894.

[47] Kreps, David, and Robert Wilson, 'Reputation and Imperfect Information,' *Journal of Economic Theory* **27** (1982), 253-279.

[48] Ledyard, John, 'Information Aggregation in Two-Candidate Elections,' in *Strategic Models of Politics*, ed. by Peter Ordeshook. Ann Arbor: University of Michigan Press, 1989.

[49] Mailath, George, 'Incentive Compatibility in Signaling Games with a Continuum of Types,' *Econometrica* **55** (1987), 1349-1366.

[50] Matthews, Steven, 'Veto Threats: Rhetoric in a Bargaining Game,' *Quarterly Journal of Economics* **104** (1989).

[51] McKelvey, Richard, and Richard Niemi, 'A Multi-Stage Game Representation of Sophisticated Voting for Binary Procedures,' *Journal of Economic Theory* **18** (1978), 1-22.

[52] Mertens, Jean-Francois, and S. Zamir, 'Formalization of Bayesian Analysis Games with Incomplete Information,' *International Journal of Game Theory* **14** (1985), 1-29.

[53] Milgrom, Paul, and John Roberts, 'Limit Pricing and Entry under Incomplete Information: An Equilibrium Analysis,' *Econometrica* **50** (1982), 443-459.

[54] Milgrom, Paul, and John Roberts, 'Predation, Reputation, and Entry Deterrence,' *Journal of Economic Theory* **27** (1982), 280-312.

[55] Morrow, James, 'Capabilities, Uncertainty, and Resolve: A Limited Information Model of Crisis Bargaining,' *American Journal of Political Science* **33** (1989), 941-972.

[56] Morrow, James, 'Bargaining in Repeated Crises: A Limited Information Model,' in *Strategic Models of Politics*, ed. by Peter Ordeshook. Ann Arbor: University of Michigan Press, 1989.

[57] Morrow, James, 'Some Difficulties with Linkage in Crisis Bargaining,' manuscript, Hoover Institution, 1989.

[58] Morton, Sanford, 'Strategic Voting in Repeated Referenda,' *Social Choice and Welfare* **5** (1988), 45-68.

[59] Moulin, Herve, 'Dominance Solvable Voting Schemes,' *Econometrica* **47** (1979), 1337-1351.

[60] Myerson, Roger, 'Incentive Compatibility and the Bargaining Problem,' *Econometrica* **47** (1979), 61-73.

[61] Myerson, Roger, 'Bayesian Equilibrium and Incentive Compatibility: An Introduction,' in *Social Goals and Social Organization: Essays in Memory of Elisha Pazner*, ed. by Leonid Hurwicz *et al*. London: Cambridge University Press, 1985.

[62] Nalebuff, Barry, 'Brinksmanship and Nuclear Deterrence: The Neutrality of Escalation,' *Conflict Management and Peace Science* **9** (1986), 19-30.

[63] Niskanen, William, *Bureaucracy and Representative Government*. Chicago: Aldine-Atherton, 1971.

[64] Ordeshook, Peter, and Thomas Palfrey, 'Agendas, Strategic Voting, and Signaling with Incomplete Information,' *American Journal of Political Science* **32** (1988), 441-466.

[65] Powell, Robert, 'Crisis Bargaining, Escalation, and MAD,' *American Political Science Review* **81** (1987), 717-736.

[66] Powell, Robert, 'Nuclear Brinksmanship with Two-Sided Incomplete Information,' *American Political Science Review* **82** (1988), 155-178.

[67] Powell, Robert, 'Nuclear Deterrence and the Strategy of Limited Retaliation,' *American Political Science Review* **83** (1989), 503-520.

[68] Reinganum, Jennifer, and Louis Wilde, 'Settlement, Litigation, and the Allocation of Court Costs,' *Rand Journal of Economics* **17** (1986), 557-566.

[69] Riley, John, 'Informational Equilibrium,' *Econometrica* **47** (1979), 331-359.

[70] Rogoff, Kenneth, and Anne Sibert, 'Elections and Macroeconomic Policy Cycles,' *Review of Economic Studies* **55** (1988), 1-16.
[71] Romer, Thomas, and Howard Rosenthal, 'Political Resource Allocation, Controlled Agendas, and the Status Quo,' *Public Choice* **33** (1978), 27-44.
[72] Romer, Thomas, and Howard Rosenthal, 'Bureaucrats vs. Voters: On the Political Economy of Resource Allocation by Direct Democracy,' *Quarterly Journal of Economics* **93** (1979), 563-588.
[73] Royden, H. *Real Analysis*, 2nd. edn New York: Macmillan, 1968.
[74] Rubinstein, Ariel, 'Perfect Equilibrium in a Bargaining Model,' *Econometrica* **50** (1982), 97-109.
[75] Scherer, Fred, *Industrial Market Structure and Economic Performance*, 2nd edn Chicago: Rand McNally, 1979.
[76] Selten, Reinhard, 'The Chain-Store Paradox,' *Theory and Decision* **9** (1978), 127-159.
[77] Snyder, Glenn, and Paul Diesing, *Conflict Among Nations: Bargaining, Decision Making, and System Structure in International Crises*. Princeton: Princeton University Press, 1977.
[78] Spence, Michael, *Market Signaling*. Cambridge: Harvard University Press, 1974.
[79] Wagner, Harrison, 'Theory of Games and the Problem of International Cooperation,' *American Political Science Review* **77** (1983), 330-346.
[80] Wagner, Harrison, 'Uncertainty, Learning, and Bargaining in the Cuban Missile Crisis,' in *Strategic Models of Politics*, ed. by Peter Ordeshook. Ann Arbor: University of Michigan Press, 1989.

Index

FUNDAMENTALS OF PURE AND APPLIED ECONOMICS

SECTIONS AND EDITORS

BALANCE OF PAYMENTS AND INTERNATIONAL FINANCE
W. Branson, Princeton University

DISTRIBUTION
A. Atkinson, London School of Economics

ECONOMIC DEVELOPMENT STUDIES
S. Chakravarty, Delhi School of Economics

ECONOMIC HISTORY
P. David, Stanford University, and M. Lévy-Leboyer, Université Paris X

ECONOMIC SYSTEMS
J.M. Montias, Yale University

ECONOMICS OF HEALTH, EDUCATION, POVERTY AND CRIME
V. Fuchs, Stanford University

ECONOMICS OF THE HOUSEHOLD AND INDIVIDUAL BEHAVIOR
J. Muellbauer, University of Oxford

ECONOMICS OF TECHNOLOGICAL CHANGE
F. M. Scherer, Harvard University

EVOLUTION OF ECONOMIC STRUCTURES, LONG-TERM MODELS, PLANNING POLICY, INTERNATIONAL ECONOMIC STRUCTURES
W. Michalski, O.E.C.D., Paris

EXPERIMENTAL ECONOMICS
C. Plott, California Institute of Technology

GOVERNMENT OWNERSHIP AND REGULATION OF ECONOMIC ACTIVITY
E. Bailey, Carnegie-Mellon University, USA

INTERNATIONAL ECONOMIC ISSUES
B. Balassa, The World Bank

INTERNATIONAL TRADE
M. Kemp, University of New South Wales

LABOR AND ECONOMICS
F. Welch, University of California, Los Angeles, and J. Smith, The Rand Corporation

MACROECONOMIC THEORY
J. Grandmont, CEPREMAP, Paris

MARXIAN ECONOMICS
J. Roemer, University of California, Davis

NATURAL RESOURCES AND ENVIRONMENTAL ECONOMICS
C. Henry, Ecole Polytechnique, Paris

ORGANIZATION THEORY AND ALLOCATION PROCESSES
A. Postlewaite, University of Pennsylvania

POLITICAL SCIENCE AND ECONOMICS
J. Ferejohn, Stanford University

PROGRAMMING METHODS IN ECONOMICS
M. Balinski, Ecole Polytechnique, Paris

PUBLIC EXPENDITURES
P. Dasgupta, University of Cambridge

REGIONAL AND URBAN ECONOMICS
R. Arnott, Queen's University, Canada

SOCIAL CHOICE THEORY
A. Sen, Harvard University

TAXES
R. Guesnerie, Ecole des Hautes Etudes en Sciences Sociales, Paris

THEORY OF THE FIRM AND INDUSTRIAL ORGANIZATION
A. Jacquemin, Université Catholique de Louvain

FUNDAMENTALS OF PURE AND APPLIED ECONOMICS

PUBLISHED TITLES

Further titles in preparation
ISSN: 0191-1708